WOVEN WORDS PUBLISHERS *presents*

Bit of Soul by Nandini Rawat

What is Bit of Soul all about:

"It's all the bits of ruminations,

all the parts of life,

all that we go through,

all that we face,

All that we feel, and

All of the thoughts

A mix of every bit of soul, heart and mind

Put into words.

So, in plain words, it's every bit of life reflected in poetry and prose.

Hope your bits of soul connects to my bit of soul!"

Bit of Soul

Nandini Rawat

Woven Words Publishers OPC Pvt. Ltd.

Registered Office:

Vill: Raipur, P.O: Raipur Paschimbar,

Dist: Purba Midnapore, Pin: 721401,

West Bengal, India.

Branch Office(Operations): Hyderabad

www.wovenwordspublishers.com

Email: publish@wovenwordspublishers.com

First published by Woven Words Publishers OPC Pvt. Ltd., 2018

Copyright© Nandini Rawat, 2018

POETRY

IMPRINT: WOVEN WORDS FIRE

ISBN 13: 978-93-86897-47-3

ISBN 10: 93-86897-47-4

Price: $ 25/₹350

This book is a work of fiction. All names, characters, places, addresses and incidents are fictitious and product of the author's imagination. Any resemblance with any events, locales, persons-living or dead, is purely coincidental.

The author asserts the moral right to be identified as the author of this work.

All rights reserved. This book is sold to the condition that it shall not, by way of trade or otherwise, be lent, resold, hired out, or otherwise circulated without the publisher's prior consent in any form of binding or cover other than that in which it is published and without a similar condition, including this condition, being imposed on the subsequent purchaser.

Printed and bound in India by Woven Words Publishers.

Printed and bound in US by Amazon.

ACKNOWLEDGEMENT

Before we start reading and relating to my words in poetry and prose.

A BIG THANKS TO YOU FOR OWNING THIS BOOK!

I TRIED MY BEST TO MAKE IT RELATABLE.

PLEASE feel free to share your most liked writing of mine and spread the word about it!

THANK YOU VERY MUCH! YOU ARE AWESOME!!!

I want to Thank special people in my life. This is my first book so bear with me,

The list is a little long, but I will try to keep it short.

Firstly, Thanks to my Dad and Mom.

Sisters & Brother < Deepika, Padma & Tilak >

All my Cousins, friends and well-wishers – THANK YOU ALL!!! Lots of Love! ♥

Special Thanks to Arshita Singh and Woven Words Publishers.

And All the beautiful souls, I would like to thank each and every one of you, who has always been here and there but still believed in my writings, supported, liked, shared and got inspired, which in turn inspired me to keep going. Also, thanks to those who low-key connected to my writing but didn't share or ever liked for personal reasons, which I am sure will get better with time! LOVE YOU ALL! Thank you! Each one of you INSPIRE ME!!! ♥

CONTENTS

FAMILY: *First things first!* — *8-17*

FRIENDS: *One and of All kinds* — *19-22*

CRUSHES & BLUSHES: *One where can't stop smiling already* — *24-30*

LOVE: *One which comes after crush, literally!* — *32-56*

RELATIONSHIP: *One that happens after, you know what* — *58-67*

HEART-BREAK: *And so it happens!* — *69-78*

BROKENNESS: *And it continues* — *80-95*

MENTAL HEALTH: *One where I can relate to you* — *97-110*

HEALING: *One where you re-discover yourself!* — *112-124*

SELF-LOVE: *One for yourself - The real love!* — *126-137*

SELF-CARE: *One that comes after real love - Duh? Cuz you gotto!* — *139-143*

SELF-RESILIENCE: *Once and for all – Cuz You are worth it!* — *145-158*

CONCERNS & ISSUES: *and this keeps happening around!* — *160-188*

SHE: *One with a little more focus on!* — *190-200*

MIXED Emotions: *One on all kinds!* — *202-220*

LAST!!!: *I promise! - One where it all's done! (Inspirations and light small poems)* — *222-234*

SURPRISE!!!: *CUZ YOU ARE SPECIAL (Quotes)* — *236-240*

Family:

First things first!

1.

I will always be there with you...
I will be the moon on the darkest nights,
I will be the brightest star on the clear nights,
I will be the sunrise that brightens up the sky,
I will be the sunset that adds beautiful hue in sky!
I will be the rain and give you bliss,
I will be the wind and blow you a kiss!
I will shine with you,
I will rise with you,
I will be with you,
as I always said... I will always be there with you!
So my darlings, if you ever feel low,
I am there around you, you just know!
And no don't you cry,
Just look up into the sky,
Look at it for a while,
Until you see me and just smile!
You miss me I know,
It's the same with me, so,
Be brave and always aim high,
I am looking after you from the sky!
And don't you be a silly billy,
Cuz Daddy always loves you really!!!

Poem dedicated to Dad! ♥RIP Daddy!

***

2.

From the sec a new life

Breathes in her womb

She knows, that, that life

Would be worth all the pain

All the sacrifices... and,

All her love, for life.

She becomes the protector

Gears up all the strength

Profoundly educates herself more

To pass on all her wisdom.

From the sec she holds them

She embraces them,

Holds them always near her heart.

From the sec they start growing

She pours all the courage,

Whenever they fail and

Never stops feeling proud

And praises, when they succeed.

She loves them truly unconditionally

For she vowed to the universe

She will be there for them, always

In all their moments of sorrow & joy

She will let them be what they love.

Such is her love, One of a kind,

Purest, without any expectations.

For she is a Mother! A Legend in herself!

***

3.

"I wished for a Life like Heaven,

& Oh God, U gave me 'Mother'

At first, I thought U never bothered

And my prayers- U never heard

But, ever since I knew this world

Much before, to Her- 'I meant the World'

For all the times since she picked me up gently

never did I feel Lonely!

I got Love unconditionally,

and all the Strength & care-blissfully...

from all the times she tied my shoes,

to the times she dissipated my blues...

Whatever She does I always trust,

as, in everything she keeps me first!

To her I am always an innocent kid...

&For her I wish to remain ever a kid;

For everything that we shared...

the dreams, the laughter and the tears...

she always made me cheer!

Her smile brightens up every moment in every way...

Her hug adds joy in all my days,

The values that she taught...

enriched my life in ways I never thought,

In more ways than I can count...

Awesome Friend in her I have found,

Happiness, love and pleasure...

which throughout Life I can treasure!

She made my Life Heaven & Sweeter...

& Oh God! now I Know Why U made Mother!

Thank you for Everything,

On Her- Always shower Your Blessings!

***

4.

Thank You.,

For all the sacrifices you made

For all the hard work

Even when you weren't well

For all the special moments

For introducing me to the travel world

For all the strength and positivity

For all the time you said you were proud of me

For saying that I am your precious diamond

And that you wouldn't even trade for hundred million

For making me believe in me and my dreams

For always supporting me no matter what

For always believing in me

And making me believe that I will shine

For all the epitome of positivity and motivation

For showing that love can be forever and true

By being respectful and thoughtful of my Mom

For all the wonderful inspiring stories

Which inspired me to be part of one, someday!

For everything you did for us, I can't thank you more

I am grateful and blessed for having you as my, Dad!

You are my hero, my strength and will always be!

Here's something that I don't often say to you,

THANK YOU, DAD! Love you a lot!

5.

To the one who's always a thinker,

The one who acts rigid

But is full of compassion,

Overprotective towards his close ones

yet conscious towards own self,

Full of mischiefs yet chivalrous,

The one who hides his tears and emotions

that of being concerned., Passionate will,

wanderers' heart, kindest soul,

Who acts strong at his weak,

For his people to find their strength!

The one who irritates the most

but will be the first one to be there by your side!

Mothers favourite, Dads dearest, Sisters darling,

He is, still a kiddo, but without doubt

A Great Man in making!

He is, the greatest blessing disguised as a Brother!

(For that brother who is awesome)

***

6.

She is the innocent soul

The one with the spark in her eyes

She is simple, filled with kindness

The one who finds joy in little things

She has the charm of liveliness

The one with the smile like the sunshine

She has the heart of a kid

The one, also with timely wisdom

She is the star among her people

The one most praised and cherished

She creates, and spreads the joy

The one with quirky nature & infectious laugh

She is perfect mixture of everything good

The one with zeal of making everything beautiful

She is the Princess

The one who will always remain so.

(For that Sister Like a Princess!)

***

7.

All she wants is to spread the joy

She gives and gives, even when she doesn't get back

She a little crazy that way

She is the kindest soul you would ever know

She loves unconditionally

She's also a threat to her enemies

She's fearless that way

Her people are her strength

Her reason for her joy

And She loves herself too

She's a perfect example of selflessness & self-love that way

She knows to make the most of what she has

She knows when to spread her wings

She's one of a kind that way

She's a fairy!!

(For that Sister like a fairy)

***

8.

Last glance. Last words.

Last hug. Last Goodnight kiss,

from you, my Dad, my Hero,

never had the last chance

to spend time with you.

Now there is this wall of fate

So.. Strong, it makes me weak

Unbreakable, it makes me numb

Invisible, it makes me lost

But it's transparent for you

So, I know you are there

Even when you are not

In all my last and firsts

Like you have always been there

As my Hero, as you were and will always be.

***

Friends:

One and of all kinds

1.

Hug is love

Hug is unspoken affection

Hug is relief for broken

Hug is essence of friendship

Hug is healing for depression

Hug is assurance for wrecked

Hug is sign of communication

Hug is exchange of compassion

Give it to the one who need it the most

But be sure it is heartfelt,

And you will be amazed,

how so little gesture has its affect, cuz,

Hug is power!

***

2.

After everything and all the time

Of good and bad, of fun and silence

I have become hopeless

and yet at the same time

I still hope that someday

Someday we will all

Cross our paths in our lives

And we will all come together

Forgetting the past

Letting go the toxic and worst

Be people or be matter

Just holding on to the good,

The fun times and the great ones!

And maybe...

we will all create some more awesome ones...

And be awesome together... like we were... (Friends)

***

3.

Whether you feel okay or not okay

There is always one companion

That would make you wonder

With all of its magical stories

It fills you with every emotion intricately

See and also feel at the same time

Get lost in a beautiful world of imagination

And just in no time you are living...

Living among each and everyone

that you fell in love with,

And dying to know more about them,

And when their story ends..

You are filled with an experience of lifetime!!

It never gets old with its stories to tell you

Instead you get closer with every new story.!

It is your friend for life and stays forever

Unlike people! Because it's better than people

It's 'Book' - your Mind Soul's true companion!!

***

4.

Somewhere between..

Being caught up with

Fake friends, fake love,

Lies and all the fake drama,

..And realising the truth,

We lost the real friends, real love,

and also maybe a true soulmate!

***

5.

Sometimes you gotto grow Thorns around you,

just to see how many actually care to

 take the risk to have you in their life!!!

-Of friendships and relations.

***

Crushes & Blushes:

One where you can't stop smiling already

1.

I see a vision and at the moment

It always stops at you.

I couldn't figure out if it's you

Someone I already knew,

Or someone new!

For every time it stops at you,

I can't see your face but just flares

It goes tripping in round and rounds

In light and shine

Every now and then

Making me a prisoner of your thoughts

In which I never aim to get lost.

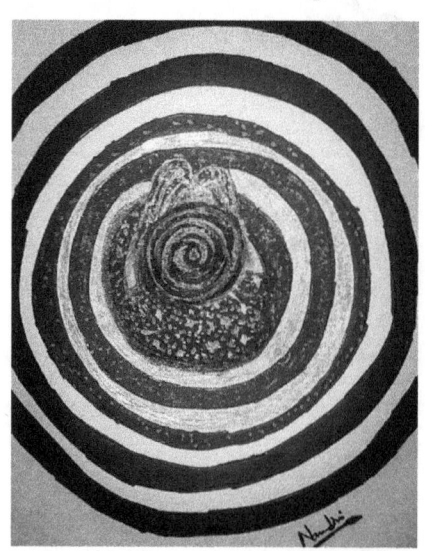

***

2.

Oh hell! so many boundary factors

Than the so-called bonding factors

But if we get lucky and the time offers us

One day, the whole day of just us,

I would take a chance at it and

Entangle in those rosy sweet

Source of the honey dripping words

Take a dip in those dreamy eyes

Fall into those soft glowing arms

Feel the touch of your skin

Warmth of your blood

Fierce passion in your bones

Then merge into your soul and

Live an eternal life in another dimension

In those few hours where we get lucky

Where our love is the only existence,

The only truth, the only factor that matter,

And all those boundaries just fade away.

***

3.

Oh boy! Look away!

Don't look at me like that

With such dreamy eyes

You look like my new woes!

I am in sagacity of my own depths

Floating in the light in moments

And when I look at you, when you look at me

I see your soul, finding for surfeit of answers

I sense you are broken too, too many a times.

Seem so ready to drown, without a care in the world.

But honey, let me warn you,

When the hurricanes will hit and

Break the glass of patience,

I mastered to float along galaxies, and You!

Dear, you gotta earn to hold my hand through.

***

4.

Girls, if He

Opens up to you

Talks about life, stars and

Everything that matters

Little and big things

Sheds tears with you, for you

Treats you better than all

Hang on to him, because

That sensitivity level is rare

And if there's connectivity too

It's worth to have someone like that!

Because emotional connection is sexy.

***

5.

I see you

And I am lost

That smile

And my heart smiles

Those eyes

And my eyes sparkle

That laugh

And my face blushes

That voice

And my heart pounds

I think about you

And I smile effortlessly.

You are my superstar

And I am you super fan

You don't know me

And I doubt we would meet

Maybe, someday we will

They might call it madness

But for me it would be a

Magical dream come true.

***

6.

With my eyes closed or open,

Near or far, always in my head and heart,

Connected in my soul too,

It's just you, only you!

***

7.

Her eyes when set to past

Still seek for the love in his eyes

for that one look, one moment

One sec of eyes full of love for her.

***

8.

Didn't believe that the broken

can feel and fall again

Until I saw that pretty face!

Oh, such pretty face!

With Scintillating smile

***

9.

I look at you and the time stops,

every time it's like that first look,

that first moment I fell for you,

that look of forever in your eyes,

that has been through all this time,

will always be now & forever!

***

Love:

One which comes after crush, literally!

1.

Those golden rays

That view of solace

That moment of warmth

The golden aura when formed

Freezing the moments of longing

To a sense of belonging

Filling the void in heart

With its own palette of art

And all the beautiful hues

Gold, orange, reds and blues

Such is the beauty of Sunset

Creates Serene Perfect moments!

Everytime in you! With its remarkable view!

Of Sunset and love

***

2.

In this shallow weird world

Of all decorated and plastic ones

Be the exhilarating wild flower

That destines the search of a Wanderer

That one, few of many

Found in the heights

Far of all the sleights

where it blooms only,

when it's touched boldly,

By a soul that of a compassionate

That whose rawness is truly admired

For all it's perfectly uneven petals & thorns

But not plucked out of its roots

Letting it grow, with all the love and respect, constantly

Unravelling the intricate essence of life, consistently

Without taking away the life out of it.

Of love & reality

***

3.

Hold her arm,
Bring her close,
Close enough to feel sweet aroma!
Wrap your hand around her,
Hold her Tight,
Tight enough to feel her warmth!
Hug her tight and nice,
Bring her even more closer,
Close enough to lock your lips!
Lock it subtle and nice,
Fall in love with her all over again,
Feel the kiss like first time, every time!
And the freshness of the first sip, Aromatic relief with every next sip!
Because She's Best of the World!
She is a Therapy! She is Coffee!
Coffee is Love! Coffee is Life!

Of Coffee & Love

***

4.

Like the parallel waves, parallel lines, parallel galaxies, universe's collide

Just like the sun and the moon during the rare rare eclipse,

Even for moments of eternity.

Let's collide too on our parallel times of life!

***

5.

Of Feelings and reliability

I wouldn't relate to the feeling
A feeling that's new
I ask myself what is this?
Why is this happening now?
I haven't been there
Why am I being diverted there
There to the memory lanes
Where I didn't want to go
I didn't want to relate to
I didn't want to be
Which I have tried hard to
Forget and leave back
Back in pieces as it left me
Is this the feeling the same
The feeling that I can't relate
Also relate to at the same time
Once which I did to
Once where I have been
Once where I did dive in
I wouldn't know!
I wouldn't know
The feeling of rush
And the pain and of those
All hush and blushes
Of all those notes
Looks and talks
And of all those times I spent with him, once
Is this the same feeling?

I just couldn't figure
Maybe! Maybe because I don't want to!
For I know, I know the feeling that I relate to now
Is the feeling once drowned me and made me lose me. (Protection)

***

6.

I like quiet places, empty coffee shops, less crowded places! I like sunsets, the full moons, the starry nights also a clear sky! I like the clear waters, the sound of waterfalls, the rain and the tapping music of raindrops! I like beaches, the loud waves, the hard splashes and the playfulness in seconds of swirling wave over my feet, then the moment of stillness when waves settle in! I like the silence, the sad notes, the high low notes, the electro, the Sufi, the psychotic ;) the trance, the loud music of my fav tunes too, I like to sway with the tunes in groovy moves! I like to get lost and travel a mile while sipping my tea, visit places, add new characters through a book! I like straight talks, transparent moments, accountability of actions, whether right or wrong! I like you, if I ever say so, then baby don't just be but live up to it, don't just give me your heart like any, but bare me your soul, don't just say things about you but talk to me about your demons, don't just take me out but make me travel in the universe within you, don't just tell me that you like me, but show me through your eyes, don't just hold my hands, but hold space for me in your empty spaces, don't just tell me about your thoughts but every figment of your brain that makes you trip within, don't just sip a coffee with me, but swirl the stardust of your aura and get me drunk on it, don't just let me sit beside you but let me get lost with you in your silence, don't promise me a forever but take me on an eternal ride of together even if it's in moments! Because that's what I will do with you! But if you don't stay by it, if you don't value the authenticity of my soul, and not understand the essence of vulnerability, you will just be one of those faces in the heavy crowds and I won't even pass by you, for darling as I said, I like quiet places, empty coffee shops and less crowded places.

***

7.

I try, try to look at you looking at me

Get caught in to your eyes and the trials you make to make some trials to look at me while looking at you and smile.,

And when I see you, you just pass by me

You do not look or smile or

look if I am looking at you

Then I blink my eyes,

Only to come out of a day dream

Again I see you before me

I try looking at you,

You looking at me and smiling

Then again you come close to me and

just pass by me

I blink my eyes again

yet again I come out of the dream of the day dream,

It keeps happening in loop, again and again,

Every time you come a little close to me and the dream breaks.,

Until I am out of the zone of you.,

Where every time I am lost looking at you,

Lost in some lost world with you.,

where you are the infinite element,

and your eyes are inception to my soul.

***

8.

Come, for a moment,

Let's get lost somewhere!

Let's go to somewhere far away

Someplace where it's just you and me and no one else

Only our talks between us and no differences

Show me your world, the way you look at it

I'll take you on tour to the world, the way I look at it

Then from your eyes to your soul

From my soul through my eyes

Let's keep on conversing like that

Some moments into our own beautiful universe

Come, for a moment, now, let's just get lost there!

***

9.

Slowly, deeply, my heart sings,

Tunes of a song weaved of,

All the words unsaid, in notes and strings,

Ruminating every thought of,

Kaleidoscopic dreams of what love brings.

***

10.

When I see you,

Sweetheart, believe me

It's like the depth effect

All my focus is on you and

All that I see is you, it's only you!

***

11.

This life, this story of ours, our lives,

What's not and what's between us

Being together and departed ways

All the love and all the pain...

Is maybe a story of a different world?

That we are watching from a parallel world

Being side by side, into each other's arms

Laughing, smiling, crying and

feeling everything together...

***

12.

There's a place
There's a universe
I Wanna go there.
There's one turn
Out there
I wanna Pause there.
A home of dreams
A world of hopes
No rules and questions
No discriminations
No differences
No competitions
Only humanity
Only Love
Only Truth and
Only Growth.
One place, one home
One Universe full of dreams
One World full of hopes
One turn of pause for self.
Love without any rules or questions
Humanity without discriminations
Growth without competitions
Truth without any differences
There's a place
There's a universe
I wanna go there
With or without someone
I just wanna walk towards it!

***

13.

While there's a story between sun and moon and how they come close once in an eclipse through the darkness.,
There's a story that's often talked less about, how the trees,
with all of its branches of responsibilities,
The growth of its flowers and leaves,
The deep roots of her love and fruits of her success also loved the sun, from afar,
just standing there, being there, looking at it, with no expectation to come close, sometimes through its scorched heat, sometimes with warmth of it's rays,
Simply loves it, regardless of its rise and fall,
Witnessing and appreciating its beauty and all the drama over the sky!

An untold love story.

***

14.

Listen, wait,
Look at me
Look at you,
I caught your eye
Didn't I?
But eye is door to soul
And I am you, your soul
Here to remind you,
You are you
Be the pain old or new
Be the light that shines in you
All from within or all ignited new
It is still in you! The light! The power!
And the colour
To remind you, your Strength, my dear!
It is You! The shine, the gleam, the pop,
To tell you again, to Never Stop!"

***

15.

After chugging on few drinks
From the barrel of thoughts
Of you and only your thoughts
I get high on you!
I love you
I murmur
Yes I love you
I nod and smile
Madly foolishly
Its true, I love you
Even before
We have known each other
Even before we met
Even before you tell me
That you unknowingly fell for me too
Just like I did for you,
Even though you and I don't talk
We converse strangely
Through the unseen unheard dimensions of time
And when we do, the time
Somehow doesn't exist.
And Every time I think of you
It's like a dream
A dream so surreal
Where you and I are together
We sit and talk for hours
Then we go silent
You get on to your passion
And I, i sit down writing a story
Then you set aside your first love for some rest
Come to me and ask so,
"Where do we go from here?"

I say the Rumi way "To the comic's and milky way
A place where there's everything we love
The stars, the planets,
Where the sky is painted
in eternal sunset hues
Where there's moon and galaxies too
All but together, of a world of our own,
Where it's just you and me
And we are deeply lost in our love
Away from the judgements
Away from questions raised
Away from all the people
Against us and our love"
And somehow it all happens
It all change's the way I say.
Then you put up your
Quirky look and with
Your child-like notion
You slide my journal from my lap
Play around teasing me
Reading out loud
in our universe of love
The love notes that I have written for you.
And then the day dream breaks
Where I just blush foolishly and
Utter to myself,
Its true, what they say,
You fall in love with thoughts,
Idea And the soul of a person
Even before you meet someone
Or even without having to be together.

***

16.

She just needed someone

To travel with her to the

Alternate dimensions

While still holding her

Close with love in reality.

***

17.

They came together

For an eternity in a moment

Just like the Sun & the Moon

During every eclipse.

***

18.

He always wondered

What true love felt like

Until depression hit her, devoid of his love.

He knew then, it wasn't for faint hearted, like him.

***

19.

Ever since I have fallen for you...

I wish I could try & find words to tell you that...

How much you mean to me...

How much I long to be with you...

How you are always on my mind...

How your smile effects me...

How your one look makes my heart beat skip...

How your touch makes me feel alive...

How I crave for one hug from you...

How much I wanna be closer to you..

How much happy I am when I see you happy...

How special I feel when you care for me...

How awestruck I be when you show love...

How my heart throbs when you kiss me...

How everything else fades away when I am with you... &

How much I wonder if you feel all that too...

I love you so much that words can't explain...

I love you too much that can never be measured...

***

20.

And when she realised she loved him

She had nothing on her mind but him

Dying to confess and at the same time afraid as hell

What if he has someone already but her

She was scared to death to lose him

And also, was set to let him go

Her heart beat skipped every time she thinks of life w/o him

All she wanted was him and nothing else

Everything that mattered in her life was him

For she knew her life would be like never before if she had him

She would be nothing less or more but only happy

She was going crazy about him

She wanted him for now and forever

Because she loved him and only him

And wished nothing but same from him!

***

21.

You, My Love, are the rarest classic being...

The charm of your smile is just ageless...

The shine of love in your eyes is precious...!!

Your love for me is imperishable gift.

And My love for you will always be unending...

Because you are my Perennial One!!!

Every sec spent with you is the best moment of my life...

Every time you tell me, you love me

Becomes an ever-lasting sweet spell on me...

With every passing sec... with every ups & downs

hope our bond be unfading... And

With every moment may Our relationship be an enduring one...

I wish it have had begun earliest

but darling...I promise it would be Eternal!!

Just like you, with your love, made me believe,

Of love and life of togetherness...

I will always be with you, for you, every sec,

every min, in every moment, keeping up with you timelessly!!!

***

22.

I don't understand your love: he said.

Sure, you don't!

Because my love for you is madness

Beyond the hopelessness

Beyond the boundlessness

Beyond the selflessness

Because my love,

I don't love you!

I love your soul more than you do!

And it's beyond your understanding: She said.

***

23.

A heart beats when two people meet.

A moment cherishes when two hearts beat.

A love blossoms when two thoughts connects.

A soul unites when love is of togetherness.

And, an eternity creates itself when two souls become one.

A True Love is two souls love of oneness...!!!

***

24.

With all the broken pieces

Distorted yet complete

With all I have

With all I can

Or maybe more

It lost but its red to you

Because that's love

Which is you to me

And it still shines...

Because that's love

Which is yours for me

So, it will! Till it beats its last!

***

25.

They don't talk to each other

But their hearts converse

Through their stories.

***

26.

You are the best painting that I could ever depict...

You are the best of all my dreams that I could ever attain...

Your smile is the best music that I could ever listen.

Because when it plays, the world goes on the mute...!

You kiss on my forehead and everything is at peace.

You look at me and I could see my reflection shine...

In your eyes so deep

That the world takes a pause!

You touch your lips with mine

And all I could feel is pure bliss...!

You take me closer and hold me tight...

I close my eyes and still it's the beautiful sight!

I may not tell you this every time we meet...

But every time I see you my heart skips a beat!

Every time spent with you is the best!

Everything about you is simply best!

Best is the only thing that could define you...

Because You are the best thing ever happened to me...

And you will be my best till I take my last breath!

***

27.

Everything you love might not give pain

But every pain you feel comes only from love,

Love that is deeply anchored in your heart,

Love chained to the eyes of your soul!

***

28.

Buy me a ticket to a parallel universe where every beatific moment spend with you is a hundred thousand years!!

***

29.

Wrapped in your arms,

Every bit of my soul ignites, and,

Phoenix rises through ashes, facilely!

***

30.

Love is nothing

But a sweet lie

That we have all been told!

That we all drive through

In Journey of life

Showing up signs

For some a little early

For some a little too late

And in that road of destiny

Which everyone travels

Taking Turns on streets of truth

Gaining different perspectives

Of some to live

Of some to die

And of some

To live while dying every day!

***

31.

And they kept swaying to the song of their souls, forever!

The melody of their hearts synced to the same pitch,

It's when they hit the notes creating their own tunes together,

Their own Music of love to dance for life...

***

32.

Dream is, of a love, affection and pride of his,

To be treated as a special part of his life...

He ever had, has, and, will ever have,

To be as his own self till my last breath!!

And if it's written to happen the dreamt way,

Only even for a day, then I wish,

Death comes to me the very next sec that day ends..

Ending up as eternal love,

that of a happiest and peaceful soul!

***

33.

If you have to travel,

Travel through my heart to soul

For You will see the world I dream with you.

***

34.

All I wish for is a "Happy True Love",

Of a simple love which would be more than ordinary,

Some love that could make life worth-living,

Some concern to make me realize my carelessness,

Some respect to vouch in my self-worth,

Some honesty to know that it still persists,

Some attention to the detail, did by, got by, none.

Some affection to boost up the confidence in me,

Some nurturing just to remind me the kid in me,

Some priority which is never less than others!

Some share in life to be felt his,

Some small lil acts to show I am his pride,

Some things done without being asked, without being said ever,

Some lil surprises that would take me amidst the stars,

Some lil ways of naughtiness to keep up the warmth,

Some of everything and less of nothing..!!

***

Relationship:

One that happens after, you know what

1.

Dearest, I don't want your riches,

I don't just want your smiles,

I want you to let me hold you,

I want you to let me be your friend,

I want you to make me your ally!

I want you to let me drown in the depths of your oceans,

Make me part of all your sorrows and pains,

Let me cry with you, let me hold you when you do,

Let me just stay in your silence and in your words too,

I don't promise to make you swim all the way up,

But I promise to never leave your side!

I will let you take all the time,

Then, when you make it ashore,

I will give you all my sunshine,

Just to see you the happiest,

I don't want your praises,

Just a promise,

To not leave my hand, when I get tired,

When I get absorbed

With all your demons or mine!

***

2.

He kissed all her moles,

She kissed all his scars,

Love kissed all the

Bewilderments,

Forever kissed all kinds of

Good-Byes!

***

3.

Think of me and I think of you

We are thinking of same

At that same moment

We are together

And beyond all they we know

And that we don't know of

We are with each other

Beyond this planet

Beyond the universe

Beyond a place that's not known yet

Beyond what we know about ourselves

***

4.

Some stories never end
'cause they never begin.

You! Yes you!

You know who you are

You know who I am

For you are in me

I am in you

You and I

We are in each other

Within and with one other

Through the thoughts

Connected with the inceptions

We don't even know, exists

We don't even talk, ever

But we converse endlessly

I dont know you

You don't know me

But we still are interwoven

In this strange cosmic connections

We, create our stories,

Meet, in the loops of time

In a lost place, another world

A space Which exists parallelly

Bit of Soul | **Nandini Rawat**   @rawat.sn

In the mist of stars

In another galaxy

A land of clouds

A Million hues of sky

So so far from each other

But always so close together

Like Almost, I hear you, I feel you

You touch me with the fragrance

Of that unknown but very familiar

Like you are in my bones

In every particle of my nerves

Living, breathing and sensing

Falling in each other's arms

Touching and feeling the sweet nectar

Of those soft lips, smiling and caressing

Yet I don't know how you look

Neither do you,

But we are intertwined strangely

In a beautiful place of our own

That we call, home

Our souls, our consciousness

Away and different from reality

Holding hands, of so proximity

So real to be true

So true to be real

Maybe it is

Maybe we are

A feeling that we are living

Maybe, you in my dreams

And I in yours!

And our story will never end

Cause our story would never begin.

***

5.

Treat me like an option and

I'll leave you with no option!

Treat me as a priority and

I'll show the world your priority!

***

6.

You can damage someone

Who loves you truly

To a level that you can never imagine

It might sound silly to you

But for them it's their reality

The heart that they put into you

The soul that they would trade for you

The mind that only thinks about you

Everything you do effects them

Good, bad, right or wrong

It does to the ways that you can't think of

To the depth that you can't feel of

To the places where your thoughts don't travel

It stirs their soul and breaks their heart

It ghosts their mind and tear up their belief

It kills their hopes and sometimes even them...

So when you get so lucky

To have someone who loves you truly

Do everything right from the start

From little to big things with nothing

But only, love!

Because it matters,

It matters more than you realise!

It uplifts them more than you know!

And you wouldn't want you

To go through all that trauma,

Then why be the cause?

Be all in or just don't be!

***

7.

Through thick and thin

Through dark and light

You are always there.

To hold me and walk me through!!

It will get cloudy and

It will be sunny too.

Will be rainy and just simple.

With a serene view...

Because by my side, it's always you!!

Not hoping it to be a plain,

Or a hassle-free way,

Of just roses and no thrones,

Of only calmness and no storm,

And of what it is and it will be.

With love and with all its beauty

We shall pass through all... Because,

Whatever it takes I know,

You will be there for me,

And so, will I, always!

Because everything with you.

Just feels right!!

***

8.

You are so much like me

And I am so much like you

The likes. Dislikes.

Love. Passion. Hate. Ego.

Same fire, same desire in the heart.

The world. The people. The denials. The acceptance.

Same perception, same connection in the mind.

Happiness, Sadness, Care & Respect.

The breaking point, The freezing point.

Same take, same resolute on things.

Time, Patience, Honesty & Value.

Same of everything and same of nothing,

Same for you and same for me.

Yet different in understanding...

Different in understanding the sameness...

Understanding ourselves,

We will understand each-other,

Someday, Maybe!

***

9.

The cold vibes from your body.

Scintillating lights of tingling sensation

Entwining the cold wires so deep, we feel.

***

10.

Take me to the moon

Show me the stars

Dive with me into the milky way

Sail me thru the black matter

On the other side of space

A place build on the dreams

Decorated with breathing flowers

Play the music of planetary hymns

Dance with me on Galaxy

Hold me tight and hold me close

Whisper all the words those

You always say to me,

"Darling, you are my everything,

And to lit a smile on your beautiful face,

I will do anything, to fill your hearts empty space!"

***

Heartbreak:

And so it happens!

Bit of Soul | **Nandini Rawat** @rawat.sn

1.

From now on I won't blame you, anymore!

It was me who forgot that,

This world has got so many liars,

And my love, you were just

One of them!

***

2.

She Knows about him

He knows about her

But not through each other.

Once, they who thought

They were made for each other.

***

3.

It was a Sunny day when we first met

Then through all the storms and on Cloudy night

We lost each other on the different paths

Like we found each other on a same path

Though we couldn't, now, be together

I wish alone at this moment, that we never met, then!

***

4.

About the times, from the sec even before I open my eyes in the morning, till I rose from bed, while sipping the coffee, checking my phone, eating, listening to music, reading a book, while among people, while with you or alone, watching something or doing nothing at all, while working, or just sorting out something, when talking to someone or just to myself, when I am happy or sad, to the last sec before I close my eyes and fall asleep, at 3pm or 3am, all day all night, everyday, I just couldn't stop thinking about you. They say you truly love someone when they are all you think about. You were that to me. I thought I was that for you too, it was what you made me believe. But you were derelict towards it, and I would still think of you all the time, this time you became the reason for all my sufferings, cuz honey, when your heart breaks in true love, it damages the soul, and you wouldn't know it ever but I hope you do. Someday. And now that I am off you and budding from all the damaged bits of my soul. I say, Thank You, but you lost it all, when you had it all. Sorry for your loss. Truly.

***

5.

I waited for you all through the winter
All through the rain and withstood the storms
Waited through all the blooming flowers
All the falling leaves
Under the shining stars and moonlight
But love, you only came through
Like a scorching sun with all heat waves,
You were but my "summertime love"

***

6.

Today I was reminded of you,

today you were in my thoughts,

today you were hovering in my mind,

today you came in my dreams too and like always,

like in reality, like it happened, you didn't care for me, again!

you let me down, again!

you left me all alone, again!

wandering in a place of No man's land! Again!

And the dreams turned into nightmares!

Today I met sadness again,

today I lost my sleep again,

today my eyes spoke silently through tears, again!!

Today, somehow repeats, some days, every now and then, again and again!!

Maybe it fears I will forget what pain feels like!

What loneliness is, how tears roll uncontrollably and

how not to fall for false love, again!!!

***

7.

You are not the same he said

Yes! You are absolutely right I am not!

For When we started

I was full of love and now I am empty

If that's what is the reason for your leaving

Please be gone! But remember to

Never come back

Cuz once I will be over it

You won't exist for me anymore! - she said

***

8.

Sometimes I wonder

If you ever truly felt

An ounce of love

Showered on you

In All of my,

Hearts abundance!

***

9.

I never knew that one who could be the escape for the hurt and pain, could also be the reason for the same, until I met you!

***

10.

It aches, aches with all the pain, of love.

The love, she thought would save her

The love, she thought would protect her

And build her to be a better version...

But it broke her, to minute pieces

That perforated her heart through her soul

And yet with that every broken, damaged,

Aching, perforated pieces of her heart & soul,

She loved him, loved him the same...

But it accompanied with anger and fear,

She still wanted him and dreamt of him,

Dreamt of the them together,

Of the picture of lies, drawn by him to her,

She was still love-struck, heart through soul

Maybe because, her love was stronger than the hurt,

Maybe her love was more raw than the pain,

Maybe her love was truer than his existence,

Or deeper than the words said & not meant,

Or simply, maybe she loved him too much

And for her, he was her only destiny.

***

11.

Do you go back to those moments?

Where you and I were together?

Do u feel the warmth in the smiles

Like I do?

Smiles which were heartfelt

Smiles which connected souls

Smiles that made us fall for each other

Smiles those were out of blushes

Smiles especially seen in our eyes

Do you ever look at all these captured?

And given to you as the Photo Frame?

Because I do even without one!

***

12.

He created,

the boundless chaos

in her world,

And then left her,

labelling her,

insanely chaotic!

***

13.

You were my sweetest escape

From everything that hurt

Everything that caused pain

Would vanish just when I am with you

All my worries and my anxiety too

Then slowly the truth hit deep

And Love can't be without two

All I was afraid of became true

All my worries and anxiety doubled too

Of all the times of escapes and comforts

Somehow you became the reason

For all my pain and darkest nightmares

***

14.

And yet my words aren't enough for you

For you seek pride not my love

And my words make no sense to you

For you need riches not my soul

But My words are all the riches I have.

***

15.

Back to the time when listening to

a thousand years

We hummed and smiled,

feeling our love for

each other...

I could have loved you for

a thousand years more,

But you couldn't keep your promises of

us, togetherness,

Of our love, for until even

a thousand days...

***

16.

I would write a book on how much I loved you and our story,

but I am afraid, if I do so,

I would fall in love with you all over again

 and I would have to go through the pain of heart break all over again.

***

17.

I wish I was loved by you

Just as much as you loved it

So so much that

You Protect it so hard

Take care of it with such fragility

That you wouldn't ever fret to hurt me

But would never let it hurt

Yet, I never hated you

I hated the love you had for it

I am extremely envious of it, so much

That I wished to become nothing

But just it, Your Ego

Only to gain your love

Just as much as you love it

I wish I was your ego...

***

18.

At times

She couldn't fathom,

Why her heart is so silly?

It seeks validation

from the one who

broke it, in to pieces,

Pieces that she still

struggles to fix!

***

19.

That look with all the love in your eyes

Fascination and affection to the heights

You said, was only for me

And I was your hearts only key

Made me believe your words

Only to realise it was absurd

When I saw that look,

That moment of hook,

All that you said was for me entirely

For every other girl you turned head discreetly

All that even when I was with you

Shattering every damn promise of love by you!

***

Brokenness:

And it continues

1.

Darling, I would have given you my soul
If you would have just mentioned once,
My complete senses and my heart,
However, I gave it to you
That wasn't enough for you, though,
Which you hurt and abandoned
That took away half of me anyway,
And The other half didn't mean anything
If your wish was only to give me pain
Darling, you should've said so, just once
Or I wish I had the foresight about it
What is the true meaning of love, I would've shown you
And at least I would've lessened the burden of your hardships!
Darling, I would have really given you my soul
If you would have just mentioned! Once!

Of Love and Lost.

***

2.

Her soft light pillow

Turned heavy, whilst

Holding her secrets

Shared by her eyes.

***

3.

There are invisible scars that are deeper than visible ones

There's an unceasing pain that can't be explained in words

There's a wound that develops even without touching

Abuse through silence that shrills

Abuse through words that aren't meant

Abuse through actions that manipulates

Abuse through promises only to break

Sometimes it happens in the name of love.

Sometimes the relation ends in few years

But it trails for years together to heal

To come out of all the lies to accept reality

Sometimes it all starts with "I love you"

Of invisible scars and love

***

4.

My blood rush through my body!

My bones get more hollow!

The time I am reminded of you,

The moment I think of you..

Stardust within then forms galaxies,

My Soul whispers my heart to be calm.

(Keep calm, it shall pass)

***

5.

Your love was the home to my soul

Then you banished it as it was a sin to find all in you

Like it was a curse for loving you

Now it wanders deep

in the black hole of its own universe

that became apocalyptic

by all the meteor shower of pain

fired with your lies and promises unintended to fulfil, ever.

***

6.

She then collected all her broken pieces bit by bit,
And thread piece by piece, creating galaxies within,
With the power of gazillions of stars,

She knew she was the magic itself,

conquering the pain and moulding her tears in to her luminescence,

She ignited every spark with all of her love & courage,

illuminating every gazillionth galaxy bit of her soul, into brighter and glaring flare,
She became Mystical!

-Of broken pieces and Mystiques

***

7.

She was building an armour

Around her heart bit by bit

But it would in no time

Either got washed away

With her tears

Or got tear down

With the trauma

Caused with his

Relentless behaviour and

Ruthless words to her

After she gave her all to him

He seemed to be blinded

To her despondent blues, by his ego

But somehow it was claimed

To be love...

***

8.

Maybe the darkness is a lover of light,
that yearned for it,
for an eternity in its own time,
just to have it pierced for at least an inch,
and fall into light's arms,
so it loses itself and,
never returns to the dark place,
That it once belonged to.

***

9.

At times she couldn't relate to the world,

the happiness, the love and all things nice but to pain.

She longed for a kind of connection to the brokenness,

to the sadness, to all the hurt and pain till its depths.

She created a world of melancholy, a place of emptiness.

She became the abode to all the love-sick souls and they called her "Toska"

***

10.

Yes! Its true what they say

"Opposites Attract"

Just like the truth and lies,

Water and fire,

You and I did!

We are no good together

Because you are

Chaos to my peace.

So, love, I am gonna love

Myself First!

And, I am gonna love you from

The Distant,

Sometimes with Hate,

Sometimes with Tears.

***

11.

"Oh I tried! I tried but I failed!
I failed in everything that I tried!
I failed in everything that I did!
I just am done now!
I couldn't do more!
I wouldn't dare to do more!
I cant take one more failure!
I cant just go on like this!
I am giving up!
I wanna end this up!
All and everything!
All the 100 ways I tried!
I failed! I only failed!
I am all drained!
My passion strained!" -Is what you say to yourself!
But hope finds its way
In all the unknown ways
On unexpected days!
Hope is like a miracle
It brings back all the strength
It gives power such intense!
It will make you shine
It will make you define
You! Your life and design
Your dreams, that you destine!
Don't say it won't,
Don't say you can't,
Because that's a lie!
I know you can still try!

So will you please?
Please give me your word?
That you will never give up!
Never give up on your dreams,
Never give up on Your belief on you!
And Never ever lose hope!
It's just a lil rough down slope!
For it will all be just fine,
Maybe more than what you now define!

***

12.

I would be lying if I said that I hate you

Because I don't! I don't hate you!

How could I? When I loved you!

I loved you as my last!

I couldn't love anyone like I loved you

But look at the irony

You said it's same with you too

But left, cuz you never loved me as your last

And I really don't hate you for that

But I hate myself for giving you that place!

***

13.

Today I consider myself an art!

An art of nothingness!

An art beyond the mess!

For Its been days since i have done something!

It's been days since my demons

Just don't stop playing in my head

The tunes of self-doubts and

Oh, so Funny how it makes me believe

All i want is to be bed-ridden!

Some of them mischievously churn inside me, from depths of every nerve to bones.

Some talk to me in such a continuous flow that i almost go deaf to the one speaking right next to me.

I feel the tap on my shoulder asking - "hey are you here?"

Now what do i say? No i am not! I was lost among the loud roars of those feeding inside me, telling me,

How insufficient i am!

How useless i am!

How unproductive i have been!

How worthless i am to any single soul!

How i wouldn't be able to do any stuff, even if i want to!

Bit of Soul | Nandini Rawat @rawat.sn

How i should avoid everyone and just be inside the closed room, on the bed all the time or maybe even better in a dark corner!

How the dark, blank, faceless, shapeless, demon, hover upon my head, engulfing all the positivity!

How i should rather lose hopes on life and stop living than trying!

Or-maybe how i fight with them every sec!

How there's been so many space wars, world wars and nuclear wars within me!

How the parts within me is lost, forever like those missing hopes and dreams in Bermuda triangle?

Or how the world has stopped and fallen apart losing its gravity?

Or oh maybe how the galaxies have been disappearing inside the black hole, like all pitch dark black!!!

In endless loops, repeat mode, again and again and how it all plays again REVERSE on and off!!!

I just don't know how to put it in words, to make 'em understand, and even if i do so, i highly doubt they would understand, so I just say - NOTHING!

That moment I wear my heart on my skin and soul in my eyes, apply possible layers of filters and make an art on my face as - Smile!

And everytime i only end up saying - "Nothing" "I am listening" and mostly, very importantly tho that "I am fine" yah.. "I am fine" maybe that's the art of being, living and dealing, when you have demons living lease-free within, accepting that you are an art of mess of shine and darkness like day & night!

14.

With her wing broken
Dripping blood out of her scars
With one hand she draws power from her own universe of soul and conscious
With another she creates a new One,
She infuses the power from the universe within,
Mending her bone marrow with her own "love" that she had forgotten to give herself,
She lets her broken wing tear down in feathers,
Sending those in bit and pieces
for those who waits for an angelic sign,
With sheer cosmic magic of "hope"
she regrows her broken wing,
That is how she surpasses the brokenness!
Every time someone thinks they have broken her enough,
She surprises them with her mighty wings that shines of stardust,
And grows every time a little bit larger than what they have witnessed.
For she is celestial spirit of divinity humanely manifested.

***

15.

I have stopped searching for you,

All those promises that you made,

All those words that you said.

I have stopped thinking about,

All those memories of yours.

I have even forgotten about you.

But, there's this thing this one thing,

I couldn't forget, I still am unable to leave behind,

I just can't fathom yet until this date...

Why would you even express that you love me,

When you never had any intention to give me any love?

Once the moon had disappeared...

And the darkness prevailed again,

With shattered new hopes & beliefs,

She paused. Scared and broken...

Yet again she had lost, the one she had.

In despair she was. Deserted and lost...

Choosing her journey to cont. alone.

Towards the darkness, she walked,

Away from the moon and it's light.

Giving up on her hopes, and dreams,

With her smile on just for the world,

to meet Life at its darkest possible point.

***

16.

She was so drunk in his love

That in that high

She could only think of happy times

Of him and her, together, every time

But when the painted glass of lies broke

Blowing the shattered pieces on to her

And few piercing into her skin deep

Hurting and Oozing blood

Leaving the scars that doesn't fade

Now she gets drunk on the spirits

And all she gets is painful thoughts

Thoughts that rewinds and repeats

To the time when he called her his love of life

And then spoke high of a wrecker

Making the wounds and scars, mutilate deeper

***

17.

Most of the times I am lost in thoughts

After we lost each other, wondering

If you ever loved me like I did?

And if u did, if you still love me like I do?

If you do, if you still miss me and

Think of me, us, what we did, how we were,

Those happy times, those moments of love,

How we would be happy if things wouldn't have gone wrong,

How we would have each other like we always wished for,

How serene it would've been if we were just together,

Even when we aren't doing anything,

Of all the future and life together,

Of every detail and dreams building?

And if you do think, do you also get the smile

Like I get?

And then suddenly

it turns into a long heavy sad sigh

Because all those are not real

But just the "if" story of our life!

***

18.

Now that you're leaving

Please give me back...

The hopes that were shattered,

The dreams that were broken,

The trust that was crumbled,

The time that was never valued,

The feelings that were crushed,

The thoughts that were damaged,

The love that I gave you all,

And most of all

The me that I was before you came!

Can you?

I know you can't!!

But there is something that

You can give me,

'Peace' by leaving me with 'truth'

Only truth and nothing else!

***

19.

Somewhere amidst

Everything and losing.

Bizarre delusions

Strikes me, sometimes,

If you ever think of us

Of all the times we were

Happy and together!

***

20.

He gave her dreams

Woven with beautiful lies,

Befallen into nightmares

Incarcerating her into the darkness.

***

Mental health:

One where I can relate to you

1.

Psst.. Psst.. they whisper

They say - we are happy you stayed up late

Hell yeah! We can play little mind twister

They say - it will be so great! •

While you worry and cry in despair

We will cling on you and make you binge

Or oh! Let's do that stuff where you just stare

Just at a wall or anything and drown and cringe! •

Ah! So happy, we all laugh and dance

The rush, pain and all that you can't take

You know you just don't stand a chance

All those who say love you, they all fake! •

Enough! I say! Enough you have said

You only come, for I feel alone now

I know I am not! Won't let you feed in my head

I don't care if you come cuz you will anyhow! •

I am healing all my scars and cracks!

And I am stronger than you know!

I don't fear! For I am now of all self-love acts!

It's 4.a.m so just hush, bye bye now, al ya foes! •

| 3.a.m. Demons|

***

2.

Save me, from the depth of my darkness

Help me, to swim above my own demons

Hold me, until I am out of the chains of pain

Pull me, out of my own grief and hurt

Let me, come back to you

Take me, back for I am losing self

For me, without you there is no essence of life

Within me, as whole, as true self

I am me, only when I have you!

Inner me, has always been conscious for you,

For I beat only in your presence,

For I, Heart, am really nothing without YOU, Soul.

***

3.

She now willingly

Wanted to be alone in the darkness.

For like everyone else,

It didn't judge her, and,

Was always there for her.

She, now like being alone

In the darkness than being all alone

Among everyone else.

Maybe it was just a phase or

Maybe it was the Stockholm syndrome.

***

4.

Dark whispers to her all the time
That she is glued down
She can't wake up
She can't get up
She can't move
She can't sleep
She can't smile
She can't just be her
It calls her in the silence
In the shades
In the lights
In the crowd
In loneliness
The more she tries to break the chain
The more it strengthens its grip
She battles day in day out
She struggles to move inch by inch
She crawls and tries to get up
She pressures against the weights
And when she couldn't go any further
She collapses and stares
at the gleaming rays
of light that calls hers out
In the silence she talks to it
Through her eyes
Asking it to wait for her
Asking it to not go away
Soul shouting in despair
That she will be out

Bit of Soul | **Nandini Rawat** @rawat.sn

She will win the dark
She will return to light
She will shine again
In next or after a million trials
But not just yet, not this one time
Not today but definitely maybe someday
For her soul is tired and
She is nothing without her soul
So for now she just wants to sleep,
She just wants to sleep...

Of light and dark.

***

5.

Failures during

D E 'P R E S S' I O N

Is the hardest

To recover

Is what the

Dark demons

In your head

Will tell you.

Listen to the

W 'I N N E R'

In you, giving

You hope and

Saying all that's

Just a lie, and

That's the only

Truth you gotto

"B E L I E V E "

To look forward

Gear up again

To get stronger

And try harder

Until you find

"S 'U' C C E S S"

6.

Some days

I fight with

my demons

And I win

over them

And

some days

I let them win

Not just

because

I get tired

But also

I do so,

so that

They don't

grow even

more stronger!

***

7.

Dear Darling Heart,

Seriously Enough Loving,

Dispirited Dreary Shadow!

Exhausted being Wrecked!

                          ***

8.

Sometimes

when it kisses you!

It will make sure,

It's essence

Stays longer

Than the kiss did!

|Insomnia|

                          ***

9.

Close the windows of the past!

If you may, visit just the good ones!

But never of the one's that's toxic!

Close it, for your own mental peace!

                          ***

10.

Sometimes to breathe is a struggle, to survive every second is struggle, for someone you know being fun around could be a struggle inside to fake it up, while battling to keep it up! Someone might not be the same they look! While every day is a new day for new change and new chance of second chances, for someone every second might be a new day for a new change and second chances! So, when you see someone acting a little different, ask if everything is fine with them, if they want to talk or just maybe be a little kind, and just be there! For sometimes just being there for someone in their silence also matters a world and maybe a life too!

This design shows a beating heart and inner love • wings flying in opposite directions for the balance in up and downs • the infinity of strength and love • the universe along, around and within
of stars, moon, sun and meteor • trailing with semicolon for all the second chances, struggles and trials to keep continuing with life and to never give up!
When my struggle got extreme I chose to get a tattoo of my design instead!

(My story to relate to your story)

***

11.

Imagine this is a place inside your head

A dark place, full of dread darkness

Where someone is breathing

You can't see it but feel it

You can't talk to it but listen to it

You can't figure out how it looks

But you still can picture it...!!

That's how depression feels.,

Like someone's breathing and alive,

Within you! Not just inside your head,

But creeping through your nerves to veins

Sending chills to your spine

Tuning your body feel like a cold winter night,

On a hot summer day, abandoned in a lost dessert.

Depression, A demon, inside, that's fickle

Sometimes fed enough of darkness,

Sometimes feeds on space and inner light!

To grow it's shadow of darkness and shine,

Through its unsightly reflections,

Pushing negativity of "will it ever be alright?"

But if it ever knocks on your door of soul!

Remember, you are not alone!

And everything will be just right!

You just have to continually fight!

And flame up that inner light so bright,

That the dark demon that feeds on it

Reverts into an Angel of Hope!

Fight! For, you and your soul are stronger than you know or imagine!

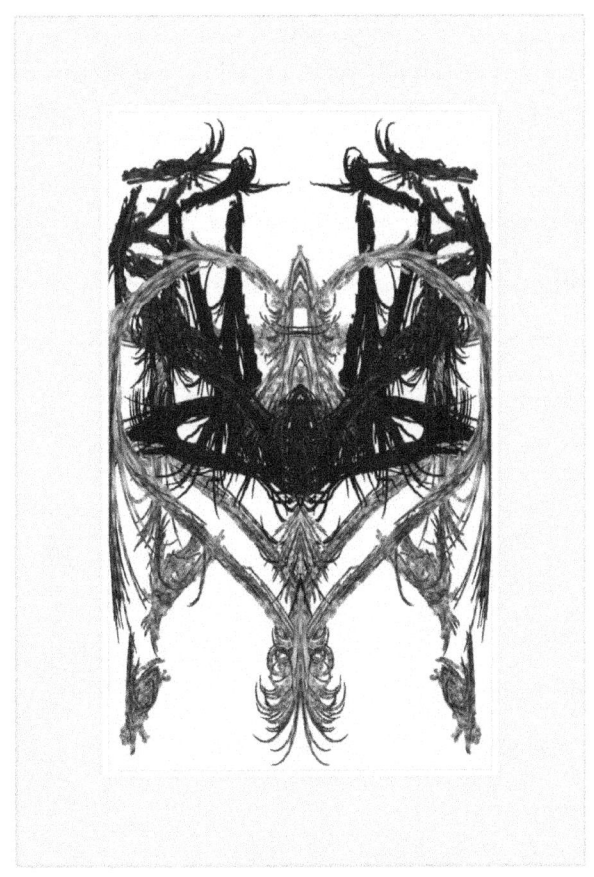

***

12.

Do not ever let anyone or anything make you feel any less!! not even you!!

•Fight with every fear and Negativity

•Pump in your self-confidence and work harder for your Dreams

•Choose to be Happy

•Be strong and face your demons in such a way that you succeed to arise above everything that you go through!! For sure you can't control everything that happens to you but

•You Can definitely decide and choose to be positive and happy,

•To fight for your dreams and succeed at Life!!!

•Most important of all choose to Loveyourself ❤ ☐

It gives you Power of Hope and Peace from within!!!!

Of Depression & Self-love

***

13.

In my head I kill you so many times

But still by end of the day and

In the darkest hours

You come alive!

In my head you are alive.

But how do I make someone believe?

When all they think that, you are

"just" in my head and not real!

***

14.

When in darkness,

don't let it shadow you from within,

cuz I will be there with you...

As the flame of fire,

Burning for a ray of hope...

Winning over the shadow,

Shining over it bright.

Lifting up the spirits high from low,

And everything to light up,

And overtake the darkness...

Even when I am not there!

***

15.

Its unbelievable that I almost

lost myself to meet you

there where you were,

Dark

Fiercely

Vulnerable

place where I never belonged,

nor will ever! Again.

***

16.

A little sneak peek of how it feels
inside the head, in veins,
When it dances
Fear laughs and grows
And it sometimes goes silent
But which also wretches
Makes you pay A heavy cost
That it pains like 1000 stitches
Leaves you empty, feeling lost!
With all sleeplessness and
Tiredness, in dire need of rest
Some days you just lose
You get no peace no option
But to make peace with it
And just pause until it stops
So you could rest and sleep
Until its back and up. Again. (Art)

***

Healing:

One where you re-discover yourself!

1.

Don't you ever give up!

Listen to the one that

Always stood by you and

Still believes in you –

"Your Soul"

For it knows your strength

"Indefinite"

As it is!

***

2.

Darling, the trick that you played,

Making me always reach you at first!

It was never a big deal! For I

Never believe in ego.

I thought down the lane,

You would learn it's unimportance too.

But you didn't. Then I stopped.

Not of ego but a thing that

You never regarded in me,

"Self-respect" and I am better off you.

For I know I am worth more!

***

3.

Don't! Darling, don't hide your scars,

Don't doll up just to make someone call you pretty!

Because you already are pretty!

Don't feel bad or sad about your freckles, your wrinkles, or those stretch marks!

Don't get depressed, Don't overthink.

About your age, weight or stats!

Because they are just some numbers!

It shouldn't be you to feel insecure with all the "ifs" and "buts"

About yourself.

Because if someone really loves you

They will love you, despite of all that!

If they don't and find reasons with

Your looks, colour or shape then darling,

Trust me, they aren't the one you should be with.

But before someone else loves you and make you feel better about you,

You do it for yourself!

Because gorgeous, you are enough and

You are worth more even with all the scars,

Within and outside and

Scars are beautiful too,

For it is part of your amazing story

***

4.

I want to be there

Where the peace is

Place where there

No distress, no pain is

Where the dreams are real

Where there's no chaos

No chaos of mind, heart or people

Where the soul finds its calmness

Through all the dire tiredness,

Damage, pain and heartbreaks

A place where I find myself

Where I find solace

Even in the void

The place where I have nothing

But resting silence

A place which will finally

After all the time in life

Make me feel home from within!

***

5.

Our heart grows much bigger, and

Our souls reach higher consciousness towards nothingness,

Beyond all the emptiness.

Every time we are broken.

When we fill all the brokenness with

Self-love and self-consciousness.

And ultimately, in our spiritual journey

We become more giving and uplifting.

***

6.

Discover being you!

I know it's so hard! So bloody hard to get up from the bed and go for something that you want to do! To clear those to-do lists that are pending since days, weeks, months or years now! It's not because you are lazy or a procrastinator, I know it's because you are exhausted, so very much and some days you feel drained all the time! In dire need of one peaceful sleep, that without any nightmares or disturbances, or any worry in the world, without the shadow of your depression, without anxiety or overthinking bugs and fears of any kind! Those demons, I know, they tell you, that you can't do it, you will never be able to do it, they keep whispering to you that, you are all alone and you will remain so., but that's a huge lie, that has always been a lie!! You know that and somewhere you have the hope, the light of confidence that sparkles in you, you know you can do it! You just need some time now, but eventually, you are going to make it! You are gonna clear those to-do lists and maybe have new lists and goals! So dear friend, just stay, maybe rest for a little more time, but don't give up on yourself, don't listen to those demons, keep fighting at least to survive, and the next level of your win over those demons won't be any far! I know, you can do it! And You will do it! I believe in you!

***

7.

Her broken pieces of heart

Of such crystalline love

Became the escape path

For the light from her soul

Through the prismic valves

Refracting out like a Rainbow!

And she shined more beautifully

Like she wasn't broken but

Unleashed into millions of diamonds

From all the darkness of distress!

***

8.

Your Failure doesn't define you, your dreams do!

You see big dreams
You try to make it true
With all the efforts
With all the trials
With every hope
With everything you have
You try, and you finally do it
But you fail!
You fail at your first go,
Or maybe again in 2nd or 3rd attempt
As heart wrenchingly painful it is
As discouraging it is to fail
As true as it is to feel like a failure
But my dear friend, trust me,
That doesn't make you a failure
That doesn't define you
That doesn't mean you give up
If you do give up, it still
Doesn't make you a failure!
There are plethora of dreams
Waiting for, to be worked on
To make it bring to reality
So what? you couldn't better at one dream
When you go check with what we started
You would know it there, you see,
We are talking about big "dreams"
One dream tried and lost
It's time for the next dream
to try and work on, and it goes on
But never give up! If you fail at one,
Cuz Your big dreams rely on you
And are waiting to be true!

So Dream on!!!

***

9.

Seeing is NOT believing

Don't just believe what you see!

Believe what you see beneath what you don't see!! Believe only what's raw, what's real, what's inside!! Don't get deceived just by the beautiful picture on outside!!! Sometimes it's just an illusion on what's outside!!

Believe in beauty inside!!!

See within you, believe in you!!

***

10.

Eradicate the negativity,
Embed the positive vibes,
Invoke the spirit within,
Lighten up the aura,
Beaming out the Lucent,
Evoked from spiritual awakening!

***

11.

When she closed the windows of past,

the tornadoes in her heart and

storms in her eyes finally ended.

***

12.

Do you ever listen to me?
Demons, try to talk!
Why don't you let me out?
It shouts!
Now when i am out!
Out of its engulfing guts!
It can't see me healing!
It says..Let me out
Let me out! It shouts!
Why don't you have any self-doubts?
Don't you wanna be of what ifs and abouts?
No! I say! I say i won't!
I say i don't!
I don't wanna be of self-doubts!
Listen to me, clear and loud!
I won't let you out!
I am gonna be deaf to your shouts!
For i have been missing me, throughout!
That me! Of nurtured self-love bound!
I won't let you out now! I shout!
But., someday when i take time-out
Maybe, i will, let you out!
I will, let you shout! Again!

***

13.

For her the world was dark.

After her trials. Trust, she had lost.

With too many strokes of hurting,

Her heart was into broken pieces.

To hope she was scared,

To feel she had forgotten,

She had lost everything in her!

Her unclear path that of the stars,

Led by the gleaming light of the moon.

Showed her the path in the darkness!

It lightened up her days to pass by...

Fixing the broken pieces of her heart,

But only to fall back into pieces...

As the moon disappeared with dark clouds!

But when she understood the cycle that of the universe...

She felt complete and finally smiled!!

***

14.

I don't wanna fall in love anymore,

For love only gives pain of all kinds!

I get blended in its colours,

Like the sea, blends with the colours that from sun rays,

I forget about my way and get lost,

Just like the sea, losts itself among the clouds,

It tells a false story and shows what isn't real,

I don't wanna be the sea that blends into colours of sun and ends being lost in clouds.

I don't wanna fall in love anymore,

For love is a liar, just like the sun.

They say sun rises and sun sets,

At different directions,

When the truth is that the sun is but mere a star!

And its the earth that revolves around it, all the time,

I don't wanna be like earth

Revolving around love all the time!

I don't wanna fall in love anymore,

For love gives only pain of all kinds!

I don't wanna fall in love anymore,

For its a liar, just like the sun!

***

15.

What is within me, will remain within me

What is not, maybe someday

What I ought not to be, won't be

I am integrity, I am power.

***

16.

Everything seems so hard and impossible

When you are hurt and numb

As if you are glued to the ground

Where you are and

Are only going down

As if you are trapped & sinking in quicksand

But it's all that pain thats making you feel so

And I know it makes you feel so real

With all the effect so real and

The hurt aching you heart and head so real

That it makes you feel that you can't move

But believe the voices in your head saying you can

And even if you have to crawl just try and

Keep moving out and ahead!

***

17.

The burning fire flaming from My heart turned coal in pain and

The fuel of my passion to not let go all that I strived for, in vain,

Heats my strength to fight against all that spine-chilling winds of cold trying to bring me down.

For I rather rise as the Phoenix than get blown as the ashes.

***

Self Love:

One for yourself – The real love!

1.

"My heart called out for you from within
It has thought of you yet again
God is witness, you are the sole happiness,
So please stay happy always, because,
Oh! I Can't take my eyes off your happy face"
I said so... standing in front of the mirror!

Of selflove and quirkiness

***

2.

She witnessed Infinity

The moment she embraced

Her darkness with self-love.

***

3.

Imagine how much a single ray of light brightens the darkness around! Such millions of rays amount to just an inch of the inner light within all of us. So when you feel weakened by your inner demons and overshadowed by the shades of darkness, strengthen your Will and try, just for a minutes or even a second to glow from within, with just pinch of courage and self-love, every time and burn away the inner demons. Then witness how powerless the darkness is when you have the power and magic of your inner light!

The miracle is you! If you think you are, you will see yourself as a miracle! And When you see yourself as a miracle the whole world, the universe and everything in life will be a miracle! Hence The miracle in life is you itself!

***

4.

Of all the years, what is been learned, what is been thru,

This time, this year, she is gonna stir the magic in her,

Of the captured stars, Of all the memories

Promises? Affirmations? Resolutions?

None into this new year! But only belief, only hopes, only actions,

Of taking care of her mental health,

Even when she couldn't,

Even when she wouldn't,

In all the little ways and big,

This time she is gonna leave behind the one, the one who would put others ahead of her,

Instead she is gonna put all the love, all the priorities, all her dreams, ahead and before anyone else,

This time she is gonna rock all her broken pieces and pour the magical dust over it all, over every pain, over every shit,

This time she is gonna glow with all the ones who truly are there for her, and love hard those who are close,

More than ever she is gonna shine like a thousand galaxies because this time, she is gonna unleash the self-love and just be better of the best!

***

5.

Of What she is and was

Today she shines
She smiles
All you see
Is her glow
Excessive flow
But do you know
Today she's on a way
She made on her own •
You see just her light
You think it's too bright
Then with judging eyes
You think she over tries •
You try to wear shades
For you can't take the blaze
Can't take long gaze
For it makes you daze •
And ponder in wonder
How could one be so pure
Such mix of strong aura
And maybe might over-power
Over you! You think - Huh! •
You don't know her reason
Haven't witness all the seasons
All the dark variations
It's now the radiations •
She was shut down
Inside a dark place
Among all the pieces
In to infinite bits
Of all her lost hopes
Of all her lost dreams
Of all her lost love
Of all her lost self •
She was lured by death
She was made to sway

And dance with the demons
All night all day•
Her soul then lit
A ray of light
She glued all pieces
Swirled darkness
Flaming boldness
In every bit together
Emitting luminance •
Today she shines
She smiles
All that you see
Is her OWN glow.

***

6.

She had a vision

A vague but a beautiful vision

Of her exquisite love of her dreams

***

7.

She is the palette of all colors put together,

also source and void of all the colors.

Of vivid vibrant shades, and soothing pastels,

sometimes bright and sometimes dark within.

On the whole from the soul to every soma built from inside to out, she is Black and White.

***

8.

While she bloomed

She let others bloom too

With the branches of her kindness

As elegantly as hers!

With her inner shine, aura and strength

She spread the roots of love

Swaying in different ways of all kinds

Empowering growth, value and strength.

And The more she bloomed

The more she nurtured

Respect, honor and compassion

in her and in all, so., she dreams,

As she blooms, to petals from roots.

***

9.

Crushed in to pieces,

Like aftermath of deep tragic!

Though she was shattered,

She built home out of chaos,

Bouldering stark wildflowers,

Of spirit shining love for self.

***

10.

She led on a way into a dessert of loneliness

But the mirage of love always called her,

Showing how beautiful a dream can be and

how fascinating it looks.

But when she moves closer and tries to feel it,

All she feels is a deep, dark, aching emptiness.

Now she walks through the mirages,

Shattering them with smirks of unaffected charms

but never stops

For she is set on her quest for the love

That's real, raw and soulful,

The love of her own

that stays strong even when alone.

***

11.

I caught myself smiling like a fool,

Thinking about you!

But then the stroke of consciousness hit me,

I was smiling, not because of you but me!

My power of imagination,

And creation of the surreal situations,

In my head, all by myself.

I don't know about you, but oh honey,

I am so fucking high on the highway of

loving myself!

***

12.

Give yourself a rose today!

Give yourself the love you long for!

Give all your heart to yourself!

Give all the peace to yourself!

If you can,

give yourself a bunch of roses,

Because darling,

you deserve it all!

***

13.

Gushing through the crowd
A crowd small but of known
Amid the twilight and lights
In to the dark lanes
Lanes covered with shards of glasses
Glasses made of dreams, hopes and love.
With the chilly cold winds blowing.
In a corner there was one
Struggling to lit fire for warmth,
In the dark cold valley, of abandonment.
Of the crowd the other
Would keep hurting self with the
Pieces of broken glass
Making the blood flow,
along with the tears,
making a pool of despair.
The other one would just stare blank,
Lost with veins popping out
relentless tiring and trying
to close eyes for one good sleep.
Then there would be one, picking up,
the shards of glasses tinted black,
And trying to fix them together,
Foolishly with river of blood into red.
Looking at them all, the last one of them,
Would taunt, shout, and laugh at them satirically.
These were the crowd of 5!
"The 5 people you meet in hell!"
The hell thats inside me!
The 5 people living within me,
The Depressed Struggler,
The Wailing Suicidal,
The over-thinker insomniac,
The hurt fool in love and
The demeaned self-doubter.
I being the care taker of hell,
I keep the doors tightly-shut,

locked strong and locked 5 times with,
Self-love
Self-care
Self-awareness
Self-respect and
Self-worth!
The 5 keys self-emerged of Soul!

***

14.

Until love finds me again

I will love all my dreams

Spread my wings and fly

To find me, love has to fly

Reach me there on the heights.

***

15.

The only real love

You will get in this

Pretentious world

Is the one that you

Give to yourself.

***

16.

No dear it's not you! You are not worthless like someone made you feel!

Someone didn't Treat you well because they are capable of only that less!

The way they behave making you believe that you are less, is not true!

I know you have pain that stirs your soul every time you think of how they never appreciated you and treated you like an option, when you made them your world!

It's enough you don't deserve to suffer anymore, don't feel any less of yourself and

that endless pain you still have, let it stir your soul and affect your heart and brain but in a way,

to remind you that there are such people who will hurt you and still be relentless,

who will say they love you but don't mean it,

Let the pain realise you how much of a better person you are than them and

how much you care about feelings and aren't ashamed of showing it!

Let it make you feel how different and courageous you are to love

Someone who didn't love you much, more and more the same unconditional way even after they hurt you!

Let it give you strength to embrace the aching reality of life and people and move ahead to be at a better place and, allow yourself to love yourself first, and be that person who truly loves you and give you what you deserve which is a lot more than what you think!

***

17.

The question is not

If he loved her or not

But if she loved her

Truly, honestly, deeply

Like she never did before

the answer is -

"Yes!" Unconditionally!

And that brings her

The sense of being,

Loving, and freeing,

From all the years of

Desolation she was in!

***

18.

When she found herself

Deep in the Cimmerian,

Of the dead promises

And barren land of love

She started blooming

An illuminating flower

Soiled with love and light

Of that from within her.

***

19.

"Your love" to me was what Oxygen is to living,

With high low altitudes in the atmosphere!

That being unstable reacted with other atoms,

Forming into what is harmful,

For some living to breathe,

Yeah, it was still useful for some living.

But you know what honey?

I Ain't no tree, need no CO_2!

And My love ain't no catalyst to hold on to

The instability of your love!

Again and again and again!

***

20.

It's so fucking strange, How we fall in love with some one. Just in no time, willing to do anything for them!! But when they are gone and we are broken, And when it comes to learn to love ourselves, accept the flaws and love the broken pieces, Or to do any damn thing that's better for solely ourselves., It seems like it's the fucking hardest thing to do... Like it's almost next to impossible but we are all stubborn too.. And we don't give up easily, bcuz we know, that, We are all broken yet we can all also heal, even if it takes forever. For, We are all imperfectly perfect in our own way. You, me, we all need to learn, accept and improve of what we are! To love ourselves, as we are the creators of our own worlds.., and there's an infinite universe within us!

Love yourself and see how fucking magical you are, but mind you, never mistake self-love for selfishness.

***

Self care:

One that comes after real love – Duh? Cuz you gotto!

1.

So honey! You want me to meet you, mid-way?

Then slowly, all the way!

But you, you refuse to climb

Down your ego's highway?

Still I am gonna

Do it your way!

Because I am a fool anyway! Right?

Sorry! That's not my way!

At least not anymore.

Its either two way or

No way!

So, I am gonna lead on my own way!

***

2.

"I don't care what you think of me.
My worst may not be worst.
My best may not be best. Yet!
But I am glad we are both doing the same.
We are both. Thinking about "ME"

***

3.

I am;

Breathing;

Surviving;

Just being;

Trying;

Working;

Loving myself;

Doing all i can;

To self love;

To try;

To work;

To just be;

To survive;

To breathe;

I am.

***

4.

In her blood through bones
She is built of stardust
Her radiant soul simply blazes
Shines brilliantly a billion times more
In dreaded darkness!!!"

***

5.

Girl, don't!

Don't get back with someone

Just because he is a known devil

Don't settle even for unknown devil

You don't deserve any devil

You deserve a Man, A Good man

You deserve someone more than

A Good man, who intuitively

knows Your Worth. Loves you,

Appreciates you and

Stays with you, readily.

***

6.

The strange thing is I missed you all the time

When we were together

Even When you were beside me

Now when you are gone

I don't miss you anymore

But I miss me, very damn much!

***

7.

The weight that you carry around

Of the deceits and let downs

Let it go and let It pass

Don't let your history

Be your destiny

Because it's not about someone

It's about you, so let everything that hurts go

And make it about you And only

YOU!

***

8.

Make self-care your utmost priority!

Not just because you have to, but because you deserve it! The first and foremost person receiving your attention, care, concern, and love should be YOU!

***

9.

There was a knock on the door..

I woke up and opened it..

Light projected in, into my dark room

It was me, standing in front of me

The one at the door said

Come out, step out in light

Enough you have spent time in dark

All this, that you have become

Is not you and was never you

You know it too

You hate yourself as insecure and weak

So it is now the time

That you start a fresh as new

And become the better and stronger you

Come, step out and grace yourself

You know it's your inner voice

It's you who wants to save the real you!!

***

Self-resilience:

Once and for all — Cuz

You are worth it!

1.

Just like the Moon & Stars

Hides some nights but always outshines! Darling,

You will too, from darkness!

***

2.

When you use me for my kindness

I feel like a candle

And when I share my light

Let you light yourself by my

F l a m e

But then you try to blow my

Light off

I laugh at your foolishness

For Honey! I am a Magic Candle

I know how to lit myself back

Again and Again and Again!

***

3.

What no one could tell her,
The night taught her,
Silence, self-resilience and
Self-belief
That She can shine
Once again even with her brokenness!
Just like the Moon!

***

4.

Sometimes you think about
someone more than they do
about you! And when they do,
They do only to take a little
More of yourself from you but
They never give!
Cut those strings off!
Protect yourself and your
Goddamn heart!

***

5.

Your mind is the soil
for your heart and soul...
Sow the seeds of positive thoughts
Manure it with strong will
Water it with love
Synthesise it with light from within
Nurture it with your dreams
Grow the flowers of peace!

***

6.

I am a voyager

On a journey within

In a quest to know

If i could pass

through the Dark tunnels

Withstand the storm

See the light

in the end of the tunnel

Or lose track

In the strings of timelines...

Afloat above the sea

And reach the shore

Beaten up by the waves

Immobilized and washed off

Like the rare species of deep oceans and the sea...

***

7.

Sometimes the day goes really well, Then suddenly just for a sec.

That thing that troubles you the most, Hits you, pricks you from then on you try to divert get over but you just couldn't, it fucks up the whole day and the mind you set. Sometimes it fucks up and troubles you for days together and takes you back to square one, to the place where it all started and again You struggle and put all the strength just like before and maybe more to get yourself back to a functioning state. It psyches hard, so fucking hard that you almost give up! But please Don't!

Just let it be and let it pass…It's ok it's the same with most of us and You will see the sunshine and good days will be back, it may take some time or a little longer but it will, for sure, be back! And...

'The "day went well" You' will be back!

***

8.

Taking off into the skies
Into the Blue and White hues
With the unbelievable beauty
Among the clouds so dreamy
Holding on with High hopes
Pumped up with all the positive vibes
Above all the troubles and the sighs
Spreading my wings and flying high!

***

9.

When you think of me! Spend a minute asking yourself - why? For no reason you are thinking of me?
Is it good?
Then maybe I am good.
Is it bad?
Then maybe you are wrong?
Because darling, I am nothing but a reflection of you! In you! To me!
When you think of me!
It's not me but you!

***

10.

Today I am reminded to smile more. Smile often. Smile in gratitude. Smile in love. Or giggle and laugh without caring like the Young little kid. Even when I am stressed out and I don't want to, I remind myself once again and again like the little sound inside the head that urges me to be strong, I remind myself to slightly slowly move my lips to make a curve, even if it's an incomplete one, and put up a smile, For myself! For the distance I covered and led myself into the paths of tiring days, Sad days, lonely days, days when I was lonely in a crowd, days when memories haunted, days when I was alone and needed someone, or of days when I had someone but just wanted to be and not speak. I remind myself to just put up a smile and go on, for it shall all pass. And when I can't I simply look at those innocent smiles and heartful selfless giggles and those playful laughing sounds of a little kid around or once that was within me, that effortlessly brings a smile on my face without even trying.

***

11.

Listen carefully to the laugh

The talks and smoky promises

When you fall!

And the silence

When you succeed!

They don't matter!!

Don't invest even a sec 's time of your precious life on them!

Instead focus on those who hold your hand to bring you up!

And the claps when you stand!

That is the kind of people

You need in your life,

Everyone else are mere spectators!

***

12.

Authenticity is My Power
What's within me is My Truth
Of Who I am and what I am
I need no validation nor fake connections
For I have got no time for drama
Either be who you are or
Take a Detour away
Do not act it up
Do not enrage
For the wrath of my power
Won't be subtle as my smile.

***

13.

I do not know what's happening

But I know why

And still I can't change it

I can't just make what I want to happen

I am down from heart to the mind

But why am I not off from feelings and thoughts

I know how to control em

I know I have to control em

But I just can't

And I donno why

I am going down in everyway

I am letting me go down

Just watching myself drown

In the darkness of misery

I also see a beam of light

Trying to pierce into the dark

But it's out of focus

I can't locate it

Blurred and void to the heart

I do have many around who could save me

I also do have who would just watch me drown

But I need only one

That one I know will get me out

That one is ME

I have to

And I will

Swim my way up to the light!

***

14.

When she stopped dwelling

Into all that once hurt her.

Swamped herself into

All that she dreamt of!

Her inner voice applauded,

Embraced her and loved her more.

That's how she found her light

That's how she made peace with darkness.

She didn't blow her own trumpet

Among all she thought cared, But to

Only One who mattered the most -

She, herself! To blow away her self-doubts!

That's how she attained self-resilience!

***

15.

They act they love ya

They show that you mean a lot

Then they go behind your back

Create all shit about ya

Just so no one else likes you

They make peeps believe their rumours

Sometimes they do that to your family too

Because you tell everyone they are close

And you always are there for them

So they fire lies from your shoulders

Because they know, once,

Others will know your true sense

They can't shine in front of your aura

Cuz all they crave is attention all for them

Cuz all they need is praises more than you

They live for making others like them

They always try to get to know how good you are

Then They live to show off how good they are,

More than you, always tryna show they are better than you

Such friends are worst than enemies!

But little do they know that real compassion,

Genuine goodness, Truth when actually known

The glazing aura when actually shines,

That made of gazillions of stars, even less is more!

So you, my dear, you are enough on your own!

You don't need anyone who isn't true to you.

***

16.

I don't know how the closure sounds,

How that relief and how freeing it feels,

As it is never received with no valid reasons!

But the day I witness the same game

Played by the karma on to you,

What was once played on me by you,

The same intensity of pain and sufferings!

There will be tunes played as my heart beats

There will be music passing through every nerve

And steps of happy dance that soul will sway to,

That! That I am sure how it would sound like!

The sound, that would set all the broken bits in me, right!

***

17.

You left me in pieces and

Took me out of your life,

Saying it was for my good,

Like you were some typo!

Where I was overwriting blindly

Your name every time, assuring

I will fill you with nothing but love..

But love wasn't enough, you proved

It was never love for you, after all

You weren't really good for me

It was late, because I lost myself...

But this time... I will correct the typo

And type My Name...

In CAPS and BOLD!!!

***

18.

I sometimes wish if I could store

All the hurtful experiences in something,

Lock it and drop it in the ocean!

But also I am thankful that I survived all that

And came out much stronger than ever before!

***

19.

Forgot about the things I loved

Forgot loving myself, eventually

Just so I could pour all of my love

On you and only you!

But you reciprocated with pain

And only pain, too much of it

So much that my empty heart,

Void of love got filled with all of pain

Time shall pass and I shall, well,

Forget you, your name, your love

Whatever little it was,

But I will never forget the pain

The feelings inflicted by you so deep

Those scars will, I know, bleed

Everytime I feel or think of it, again,

Then, I will be ready with my armour,

Armour built around my heart

With that bled scars and pain

So I never will let it out,

will forget you or your face, maybe!

I am aware of my pain and

I am gonna embrace it,

Thank you and Good luck!

Bit of Soul | **Nandini Rawat**   @rawat.sn

Cuz dear, you know, & I know,

I am now, empowered with self-love

Filling my heart, again, and,

Selfish is not same as self-love

Coward of loving, being loved

and hence of pain too, that's you,

Before you dis, react or cuss

Be aware of that, what you

Already know... That it's true!

***

20.

For I have seen you, give your all and to take the arrows for someone you love,

To protect them, trying to make them see the truth,

Of something they were blind to,

Of something that was hurting them and you more,

For you tried to stop and took it deep into heart,

You bled for them and stood strong,

You made the devil give up,

And healed the one you love

with realisation of truth,

But when it was your turn to be saved,

When you were broken and shattered,

they deserted you, I know,

I know all your pain,

All you gave, all that you lost,

And so, I am here, and everywhere you need me,

While you are re-growing your wings of strength,

now and till the end of the time.

***

Concerns & issues:

and this keeps happening around!

1.

Grief...Truth to be told...

It never ends!

Because Grief is actually love that's lost!

The love that we feel but can't express anymore

The love that we had but never said before

The love that turns into voidness all of a sudden

The love that stays inside like a heavy lump

The love that is the reason for all thoughts to come

All thoughts that makes us get lost in loops

The thoughts that we hold within us about them

The thoughts that runs on our mind all the time

The thoughts that hits like a blank space

The thoughts that takes us on memory tour

Those thoughts never ends

Those thoughts have no words

For those, those thoughts of love

Of togetherness when they were with us,

Of happy times, of sad times, of all the times

Even when they are gone, still

Still stay alive within us

Whether you are among everyone or alone

Those thoughts never ends

And when we try to function normal,

Which we really can't without those thoughts

For sure, life goes on, it's a cycle but

When it's your dearest one

That holds a very special space

In your heart and life

You can't just let go! You can't just forget!

You can't just function normally!

Because the happy times and the sad times

Continues even after them but without them

They are always in your thoughts

Always in your heart

Always remembering them

Because you love them

And love, love is infinite and that never ends!

***

2.

Of Body shaming & Slaying

"Next time someone comments on you, of how you have grown in size and how you should rather be, look, wear, walk, sit, eat! Not concerned, if it's something related to underlying health issues! Hold them close and whisper in their ears, - "My body, my rules! STFU!"

Say it. Slay it!

Be Unapologetically YOU!

You know yourself, and your struggles that you go through, with your own body, the thousand ways you tried, the million times you motivated yourself, the infinite times you pushed yourself up to finally do it! You know, you are trying, and you are already slaying. So, don't mind what others tell you, don't let their toxic words be the reason to shake your self-confidence and don't you ever think that you are of any less worth than that "someone" with a perfect body! Because, the problem is not with you or your trials and your attitude but with the tiny weeny narcissist brain of those who try to push you down with their hurtful words, for they know & they fear that you might actually do much better than them if you had a perfect body! And what is perfect body anyway? There's always too thin or too fat! Too structured and too flat argument! Which is nothing but bullshit coated illusions to feed your insecurities! Any goddamn body size that makes you feel good and healthy is a perfect body! So Gorgeous, don't listen to any other shit! Believe in yourself! Keep your confidence so high that the shit said can't be heard! And If they still try to pull ya down, thank them with your middle finger raised high and get going! You are perfect the way you are! DGAF about any kind of Body-Shaming!! Look after yourself, and be healthy not just look wise but also feel wise and this goes to every gender, - "Your body! Your rules" Say it. Slay it! Be unapologetically YOU!

***

3.

Of Humanity and equality

Discrimination! Discrimination!
Everywhere and around
From aeons of time!
Discrimination Based on my gender,
Based on my roots,
Discrimination even based on my age,
Based on my looks!
Based on the work I do! •
I don't speak same language as yours,
So somehow you have right to call me out names,
Make jokes on the country my roots belong to,
Even when I have lived for ages or
Born and brought up in the same country as yours.
And when same happens to you in a different country,
Oh then you are the victim and it's so Racist? •
I dress up differently than you do,
I have few different parts than yours,
I bleed differently than you do,
Sometimes longer than five days,
So somehow you have the right to call me weak,
Get the right to be paid more than me,
Even when you know we possess same potential,
And in something's I am stronger and better than you?
But when I succeed it's because of my looks?
Oh then you are the victim and it's so Sexist? •
I want to be of a different gender that I was born,
or I am born with mix of both genders,
So somehow you have right to shame me,
Tease me, call my rights by yourself,
Say I shouldn't exist And when I stand up,
When I call out for my rights and deem my place,
Equally as yours, as I deserve!
Oh then you are the victim and it's so Opportunistic? •
I don't worship at all or the same God as yours,
I don't read the same verses, or follow same tradition or have

different customs,
So somehow you have the right to kill me?
Erase my culture, Erase my race,
So you get the power over me and the region or religion,
Just to make yourself seem superior,
Even when We are all but, just the dust of One Superior above,
One Universe we live in?
And when I fight back at the War that you started,
Oh so then you are so victim and it's so Revolutionist?•
Why? Why can't we live in peace?
Why can't there be equality?
When you and I are the same?
When I am or any one of any race, gender or age are all blood, flesh and bones! Same as you are!
Why can't we focus on growing compassion?
Instead of hate, ego & power?
Why can't we live with zero discrimination?
And just be A Human, First?!

***

4.

Of Period and Stigma

"Not every period result in birth

But every birth is result of period!

Birth is a personal choice

Period is not!"

So, you are a traditional, religious, orthodox,
and believe a girl on her period,
Can't enter the kitchen,
Can't be part of rituals,
Can't step in the temple!
Can't be touched!
Can't be looked at during "those days" because it's a sin!
With all due respect!
With all the pondering of why?
And back and forth rebelling of why not?
I ask you - Which God or Which verses has said so? •
So, you are a guy and you are disgusted with the thought of woman bleeding every month?
Or so pervert that you throw cheesy comments about it?
Tell me, Do you know the reason you exist?
Do you know where did you come from?
Do you know you are called "Men"
That's a word part of "Mens'es" •
So, you are a girl and
you are scared of stepping out!
Uncomfortable talking about it!
Uncomfortable asking for a pad?
Even from the other girl?
Cuz you have been said so! "It's a taboo! It's a stigma!"
Let me tell you - Please don't! Don't be scared!
Don't think what others would think!
Don't worry you couldn't do as much as others on those days,
Cuz it works in different cycles and hormonal balances!
Embrace what you get!

Cuz it's Natural!
There's no shame in saying,
Cuz that's how your body works!
That's how it supports the other nature's wonder - Birth! •
So, You are a boy, a girl, a trans!
Of any gender or any age or any race!
You are religious but also rebellious!
You don't care what they call it and
No matter what, genuinely support it!
You understand the pain!
Understand the science and it's nature!
Here's just one thing to you -
You are a Hero! Period! •

***

5.

Of Me too & Women Empowerment

With numb eyes but a courageous smile! Me too!
While it torments and the trauma never really ends!
That affects every sex and of every age!

Where few of us aren't spared even under our own roof!

Which becomes part of heart wrenching stories of our lives!

For those who can speak and for those who still can't, we hear you!

We are all together! Even when you feel weak at your strongest,

even when u feel like giving up!

We will raise a voice! And We will not stop!

With numb eyes yet with a courageous smile, we all will survive!

We will have to, us, them, her, him, you and Me too!

***

6.

Of Awareness & Sexual assualt

There will be a day I will be born again

There will be a day when you will be born again

and that day I will not torture you the way you did

I won't take an advantage of you like you did

I won't abuse you like you did! I won't find ways to

grope you and rape you like you did!

I won't make you uncomfortable in your own skin

I won't make you feel conscious of what you would be wearing

I won't tease you for the way you would look

I won't make you inferior of your shape! I won't!

••I won't let you be raped but••

I would instead be always with you and support you

I would empower you to be free and to be yourself

As you deserve and as all of us deserve equally!

I had the same aim to take forward unapologetically but

This time, in this life you found me and you

instead of being all that I just said

You were being NOT that, NOT even Human

You raped me and you killed me

You abused me and made me feel unsafe!

But I promise you

I promise you,

I won't make it so horrible for you to live!

I will make you aware

Aware of all the horrible situations

and horrible world experiences we live and face

through all the stories and build you strong and

nurture you to know how NOT to be.,

I will give you all the love and empower you so,

You love, breathe and live in humanity!

There will be a day I will be born again

There will be a day you will be born again

While I want to be born as my own self

And you as NOT my son BUT my daughter

To know, to learn and to feel a life of a Girl!

In a better compassionate way,

In a world free of evil!

We are fighting for, Now!

//rebirth/

***

7.

Of Rules and Poetry

Rules here and there
Rules about this and that
Rules of dress and looks
Rules about my own life?
My one life that I get only once?
So what if I am a woman?
Maybe you aren't aware
The most used word is She not He!
Huh what? The other day my dress was too short?
And today it's too long?
Really?
Well, oh Oops! I dropped the axe of courage,
Perfectly cut the chains of your "rules"
For your thoughts are too small,
And your senseless judgements are too long!
Lifting my dress too long, up,
Of all the mess, chaos of my own,
Embracing it as my wings
I fly in to the clouds of
My freedom and dreams,
Weaving all my words
I fly like a Poetry.
For poetry has no rules
Poetry doesn't judge
Poetry makes my chaos beautiful
Poetry embraces my mess
Poetry gives wings to my words
Poetry is courage
Poetry is dream
Poetry is freedom,
Poetry is She!

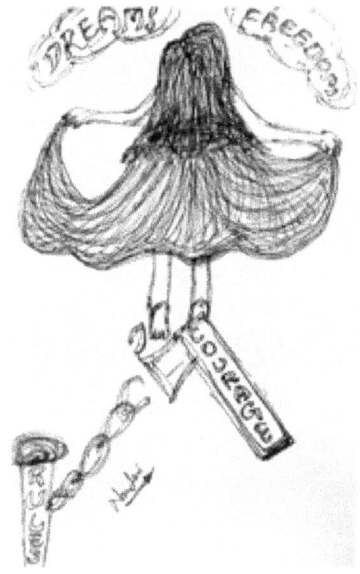

***

8.

Of Impurity and Nature

If you think it disgusts you
If you think cramps doesn't sound real
If you think it's "just" a PMS thing
If you think it's such a sin
If you think you can call it impure
If you think It's alright to treat as untouchable,
"During those days"
When A Girl is on her period!
Maybe you should re-think for,
The blood all over your body
When you were born
Was nothing but that blood
It's the same blood where
you took your first breathe
That runs in your body
Where you were for 9 months!
So, Are you sin? Are you impure?
Are you untouchable?
And oh about the pain? You should be glad
You would never know!
And if you are a woman,
And still don't empathize?
What is the stigma here?
Period or...(*Your thinking*)?

Why is Birth of a baby so Auspicious and Beautiful!
And why is Period such Sin and Impure?
Aren't both Nature's wonder!?! Thoughts?!!?

***

9.

Of Society and definitions!

Sometimes I dress up pretty
Sometimes I don't and be lame
Sometimes I wear makeup
Sometimes I choose to not
Sometimes I drive
Sometimes I decide to be driven
Sometimes I am all in
Sometimes I ain't
Sometimes I work my ass off
Sometimes I just lazy around
Sometimes I fight out loud
Sometimes I fight in silence
Sometimes I am full of wisdom
Sometimes I am silly
Sometimes I am too stressed with everything
Sometimes I am too inspired by everything
I laugh, I cry, I am crazy and I love that way!
I don't care what you tag me as
I don't care what you think of me or not,
You judge me by my race,
And when someone does to you,
You call it, only then racism,
You judge me by my looks,
You judge me by my Color,
You judge me by my age,
My weight, my work, my choices,
I don't care if you like me or not
I am not gonna change for you or anyone,
If I will, I shall change for good for me,
For I do things to make me feel good,
And not to please you!
I know that you gossip,
I know you spread rumours,
But here's also what you need to know,
I don't really really really care,

Cuz I believe in truth and I believe in what's real!
I have been raising voice against what's injustice,
And I shall do so until there's justice!
I hold strong opinions and
I will not be quiet!
I will do what I want to, what I love,
No matter whether I have support or not!
I will go where I want,
No, you can't tell me I can't!
I will rebel against society,
If they try and hold my right!
For not you, not anyone,
not my own people get the right to judge me,
Stop me or tell me what to do and not,
For its my life and and alone I can define me!!
Yes! Only I define me!!

***

10.

Of Innocent Killing & Karma

Every drop of the blood that was shed,

Of that innocent child, in tears and fluid!

Of the days of past, future and present you led,

Wait till the wheel of fate, spew up!

For not you nor me but Karma is the Co-author of life!

***

11.

"My BODY is NOT a SHOWCASE for you to GAZE!!"

"Wooho what an item!! Wow! Baybie! Sexy!
Hello! Will you come?
Heyy love where are you going?? Woah hottt! You talk? Want meet?
C'mon doll let's have some fun!!
Waaw what a dress beybiii(baby)!!
Are few of the comments that are passed at girls who walk on roads or at public places and hangout's!"
I am a girl and this is every girl different story-
"It all starts with the dirty gaze
The gaze that makes me feel dirty
But why should I?
Then I gaze back and ask the creep to STOP!•
At a young age, I am asked to come to play a new game by some uncle! He locks me up in a room and does obscene hideous stuff to me and makes me do too.
When I say No Stop it's painful he silences me and fulfils his pervert desire, anyway.
That day the child was murdered and the survived one was silenced!•
This didn't stop with my age!
The pervert levels fell so low that I wasn't spared as even a newborn and as old aged elder!•
The demons in the pervert sometimes weren't satisfied by just preying on the innocence and the body, so they would sometimes torture me for days, rape me until I would rot and die! Sometimes play with all the sharp objects, iron rods and would dissect me like my body and I am some sort of a medical subject!•
I booze, I hang out, Do night outs, wearing whatever I feel comfortable, I am just roaming around, just like the opposite gender for I believe we all should have equal right and equal freedom, but NO! If I do that I am somehow -Characterless- and length of my dress is directly proportional to amount of shame and respect I have, so they think it's their birthright to tease me, coerce

& rape me and the wonder is, these perverts aren't particularly biased towards the length of my dress or my Color! Wow! So much for humanity and equality! •
The important thing is if I am kind and outgoing, somehow, my NO doesn't have a value? Why? because in some cheesy way they feel-
NO means YES?
NO means INVITATION?
NO means Please GO On rape me??
So on behalf of every girl, I tell you this today-
You are right! NO Doesn't mean No!
NO means FUCK OFF!!

***

12.

Of Norms & "Settling" down

"Settle down" they say.

Study to settle down in job

Marry to settle down in life

Have kids to settle down ultimately

Raise them, educate them and get them married to settle them down in their lives!!

Settle down now or it will be too late!

Settle down in time or you won't ever!

Settle down for this! Settle down for that!

Maybe the purpose of life is in being unsettled! How about settle down to never settle so you could have new goals, new dreams one after another is marked off!!

How about finding the comfort in unsettling?

Let's not "Settle down" for Job, Marriage and Kid or Grades!!

Let's unsettle to new dreams, new hopes, new goals, new purpose, levelling up every time a new achievement is unlocked!!

Let's unsettle until we finally could breathe peace and joy with every breathe we take in and out!

***

13.

Of Games & Child Assualt

Sitting on the bench alone

I am lost to my childhood zone

My uncle teaching me a new game

Game which always had a different name

A new way to enjoy his pleasures

Unmindful of it, I end up in bruises

I would be numb and shed tears of pain

Suffer in silence, living life of bane

And whenever I see kids, I pray,

I wish, that they never be prey

To the games of a life burdening weigh

So I pledge to make everyone aware

For the right of every child everywhere

For, the child in me is still at war

And it will be, until there's childhood of no scar!

***

14.

Of People & Compassion

Some days, I wonder

If someone who hurts someone

Feels the same pain and agony

Why can't they understand that..

People and their feelings

Are not some toy or game board

That you play with it!

For all those I pray that

You know the difference between

Things and a Person,

From wrong to right..

Love the ones who love you

Love the ones that need love

Show kindness to every being

For kindness is the strength

Of a strong and a loving heart!

Practise selflessness not Selfishness!

Lead a life filled with compassion!

***

15.

Of Earth & our bit

Earth is abode of many species!

It's the ultimate home!

It's believed the inner core of earth is solid

Of her nature of cooling of its inner liquids

It's minerals and different elements,

And protects and shelters many!

So let's not rage it by destroying

What rightfully belongs to her

As all the creatures are it's own children

And so is the name "Mother Earth"

As it nurtures every being with its selfless love!

Let's all plant and take care of her as she does!

Protect her and let her keep her beauty!

Let's do our bit and give back some love to her!

***

16.

Of love & equality

Colour is judged with hatred

Age is judged with hatred

Race is judged with hatred

Religion is judged with hatred

Differences are born through hatred

And it all begins with a pinch of judgment

But when a human loves another human

With no discrimination

Of race, colour, age or religion

And completely out of love

Even without gender bother,

Then why can't you be human

Not judge them and just let them be?

For its love and love has no hatred

Love destroys discrimination

Love eradicates the boundaries!

Or wait is that why you hate love?

For it would fill lives with infinite love?

And kill hatred? Is that what you fear?

That you won't have power?

Such a poor human you are!!

That love is not your power!

Why dont you just let love

Win over hatred and witness the change!

Just, maybe for once step out of your bordered mindset!

See inifinity that love has to offer!

All just with pinch of humanity and empathy!!

***

17.

That's the thing about people

Who are good at sugar-coating words

They make you believe the lies!

And the ones who keep it raw

Are the ones constantly judged.

Of Raw & Sugar coated

***

18.

Of Color Red and Society

"Red" the colour of sringhar, they say. *(Sringhar - Beauty)*
Red, the colour of love!
The colour of passion, attraction and romance!
Red, not just the Color!! But a symbol!
Symbol of Marriage, tradition,
The "trademark" of women as wife with "Sindoor" in orange and mostly Red!
But in this dramatic world of society-led,
Red, somehow doesn't exist, shouldn't exist, must not exist,
In a Widows life!
Wait, that's not just red,
but all bold flashy colours from family of Red.
Must not attend gatherings,
Shouldn't have any feelings,
Cannot be part of any auspicious occasions,
If not, she is shameless and ruthless?
A woman, a wife, a lover, a partner, loses her love of life,
Her man, husband, lover a partner, the father of her child, for life!
Her companion she thought, would have till her end of life!
The life of dream to live together,
To create memories forever!
She has lost almost her heart,
Her heart skips beat with the shock.
Her lifetime hope is shattered,
Her happy together dreams have been snatched,
The life has already been cruelled enough on her!
What is that you want her to lose more?
Do you not empathize the pain?
Do you not at least sympathize the loss?
What is your gain?
Why do you want to impose harsh rules?
Shouldn't wear bold colors!
Cannot deck up for occasions!
Mustn't seem happy!
Even when she has accepted the life's fact!

When she has made peace with the truth!
When she lives for her child(s) and finds happiness in their happiness and life choices!
Why can't you just let her be?
Why can't you let her peacefully breathe?
"Wife,
Loses her
Husband for life
Somehow loses basic rights!
Right?"
Society! Oh, dear so-called society!
Why aren't your degrading, depressing, demeaning, illogical, rules, imposes, critiques, down-right stupid small thinking, not dead! Instead?
Why aren't your stigmatic stereotyping rules, aren't lost yet?
Aren't we already too late for this kinda societal change?
Or Do you not have your own life?
Do you impose same on man who loses his wife?
Expand your mind, expand your thoughts,
Step outside your small-minded rules, and live in a meaningful acceptance!!

***

19.

Stages of Women

– beginning –

-First stage-

Hi! I have just taken a shape

Maybe my first breath

Through my mother's umbilical cord

And when you know it's me, her not him,

You already plan not to make me part of your world?

Today because I have been never born

Is it why it's a Happy Women's day? In my Remembrance?

-Second Stage -

Hello! You decided to keep me alive

Let me nurture from my mother's womb

But the second I was born

You dig me a grave and place me there

Sometimes dead, sometimes alive!

You didn't even let me have my first sight!

And today because I have been never allowed to grow!

Is it why it's a Happy Women's day? As my Memorial?

-Third Stage-

Hey! It's been few years

I have been brought in to this world

Often I have seen my parents

Look at me and smile but an incomplete curve

They worry for my education, cuz I am a girl!

Worry for my dowry, but I am not even yet a grown!

Today because I have been never to a school

Or already have a husband!

Is it why it's a Happy Women's day? As adieu to my childhood?

-Fourth Stage-

Heyya! Look I am all grown.

It's my day where I hit puberty

My first time where I begin to bleed

Which of so much of blood & cramps

It's doesn't at all feel really good!

But I have been said I am impure!

It's sin to see me and or come out of a room!

I am cornered, I shouldn't even be touched?

They make me cook my own food for these days

Or give me food like they slide and throw at a prisoner

Today because I have been never treated normal during the days when I bleed?

Is it why it's a Happy Women's day? As an insult to my nature?

-Fifth Stage-

Um hi! As I walk by

The lanes or even when I am home

There are eyes ogled on me

Sometimes of strangers,

sometimes of known

They touch me, lure me,

make me do things

Or do things to me

Without the conscience of my own

For them my age doesn't matter

My look, or dress doesn't matter

Today because I have never been seen than a mere sexual object!

Is it why it's a Happy Women's day? As vale to my raped innocence and emotions?

-Sixth Stage-

Well hello there! I am a woman!

I am educated well! Or maybe not!

I work or don't it's my choice, sometimes not

I get married or not it's my choice, maybe not

I have child or not it's my choice, sometimes not

I stay where I am or travel it's my choice, maybe not,

I believe I am strong and I sure am talented, sometimes not,

But They make a choice to pay me less

They make a choice to decide I ain't strong, enough!

They make a choice that I ain't good enough,

I can't work hard, equal enough?

Today because I have never been given my right and my share of equality!

Is it why it's a Happy Women's day? As a symbol to my unequal status?

-Seventh Stage-

So! I raise my voice!

I fight back!

I don't keep quiet!

I say I need my right!

I ain't scared even a slight!

I am strong and will fight!

For that should have been my equal right!

They call me names! Say I am a bitch!

Or maybe I am just PMSing?

Raise questions on my character!

Say, baby doll this is not your sector?

They call me a frustrated feminist!

A woman who hates men! And is against!

So, today because I have never been heard or understood!

Is it why it's a Happy Women's day? For feminist is now considered sexist and not gender equality?

-Eighth Stage-

Whatever!! I ain't gonna be scared!

I still gonna fight!

I won't let unborn be killed and just be a remembrance! For she deserves to be born!

I won't let born being killed and just be a memorial! For she deserves to live!

I won't let girl remain uneducated and just lose all her childhood! For she deserves education!

I won't let girl's menstruation taken as a taboo, a sin, stigma or impure and just insult my nature! For she deserves to embrace her nature of birth!

-Ninth Stage-

Hell NO! I WON'T let her be treated as sex object and just give vale to her raped innocence and emotions! For she deserves honour and respect!

NO! I won't let her called weak and paid lesser, and just be a symbol of unequal status! For she deserves her right and share of equality!

Oh! She better!

And no, you fool! I won't let you call her names or just say she is PMSing, when she's raising her voice! For she deserves to be heard and have opinions!

Well! OK Fine!! Go on, call me a frustrated feminist!

-Tenth Stage-

For yes, I am a Feminist! And I am frustrated!

Because I haven't been rightly treated!

It's not just me but there are many voices!

That pledge all the right issues raises!

And FYI every gender, those understood

also, are beside us, with us, now along stood!

I, she and we all deserve to have an equal right!

And I won't be quiet and maybe even roar for my right!

Until the doubt is clear if it's a Happy? Women's day!

I will fight every day, every night!

Until I make it "A Happy Women's Day!"

Truly. Equally. Right!

-Poem -

She is Nature!

She is Tender!

She is a Daughter!

A Friend, A Sister!

She is a Mother!

A Companion, A Hard-Worker!

She is a Valour!

Of great Character!

She is Everything you are!

Equal and sometimes Superior!

She is a Fighter! also a Protector!

But not a victim of her Attacker!

If needed she will be storm, but will not Wither!

For She is a Superhero! A Warrior!

She is A Goddess! Holds entire universe within Her!

***

– END –

Stages of Women

She:

One with a little more

focus on!

1.

She is but just an open book.

The cover is as important as the last page.

And so are the "in between lines."

If you have no patience to

Read her carefully and mark her

Importance in your life, or,

Drown totally into her and

Be part of her universe.

Then don't bother to open her. At all!

***

2.

Let me take a minute

For you to tell this

The empire that i am building is the kingdom of a queen without a king! And the queen that you know of, you know nothing more than just your low perspectives! My empire of authenticity,

Ways of truth and pillars of boldness, hurts your nonsensical thoughts of judgements and degrading level of discriminations! Then you are not welcome! For you,

You are not even a pawn in this game of life!

And you don't matter, just realise this minute i gave you is actually all for the queen!

***

3.

Rose is beautiful in reds, yellows,
oranges and pinks,
And even in black and whites!
It's not its color that defines its beauty
But the way it is, and the way it blooms! Its beauty is in its essence.
So darling, that is what you are too,
You are beautiful the way you are,
Not just the way you look, regardless of color, shape, size and age!
How you bloom, how you careless and be yourself is what defines the real beauty. And If someone says otherwise, raise your thorns and show them the way out! (If you know what I mean!

***

4.

Her Heart revolves in phases,

Just like the Moon,

Within Her Soul as home,

like the sky!

Through emptiness and fullness

With twilights of hope in millions

Endless clouds of thoughts

Sometimes heavy sometimes light

Sometimes dark sometimes bright

And Her Mind, travels in the infinity

Loops of consciousness higher and higher

Just like the universe in matter and space!

***

5.

She had high hopes

To fly high away from dark

Now she flies breaking the cocoon

like a beautiful butterfly.

***

6.

I am a Woman Unborn,

I wanna be born, Let me be.

I am a Woman of Childhood,

I wanna be grown, Let me be.

I am a Woman of Future,

I wanna be educated, Let me be.

I am a Woman of Nature,

I bleed, Let me be.

I am a Woman of Motherhood,

I breast feed, Let me be.

I am a Woman of Status,

I want equally paid, Let me be.

I am a Woman of Mind,

I wanna be heard, Let me be.

I am a Woman of Colour,

I wanna "NOT" be oppressed, Let me be.

I am a Woman of all Kinds,

I wanna "NOT" be objectified, Let me be.

I am a Woman of Substance,

I want equality, Let me be.

I am a Woman of Freedom,

I wanna be free, Let me be.

I am a Woman of World,

I just wanna be Woman, Let me be.

***

7.

She is soft-hearted

She is devoted

She is blind lover

She is magical

She is magnificent

She is mystical hymns

She is righteous warrior

She is epitome of knowledge

She is auspicious fortune

She is unbound beauty

She is reincarnation of ashes

She is all forms of nature

She is destroyer of evils

She is supreme power

She is art in herself

She is fierce

She is tranquil

She is divine

She is universe

She is eternal

She is Göddess.

***

8.

She is just like any girl

but different with a soul.

A soul that of kindness,

compassionate, yet Strong.

she would do anything for her people

even when she is deserted and betrayed,

she wouldn't leave them

but give them chance to grow

a chance to undo their mistake

a chance to be a better person

because she believes every person

has a right to get second chance,

to learn and outgrow themselves.

but if that person still doesn't change,

she simply cuts herself from them.

she might sure be crazy about love and life

but she is equally crazy about justice and honesty.

***

9.

She had world around her,

Smiling, and kindly deceiving!

She had learned not to trust,

Not to have the world around,

Instead make a world of her own

And that's all mattered for her since then.

***

10.

Her eyes kept searching

For a lost place

Relating to a feeling

That gives solace

A place of dreams

That gives her strength

Illuminating like the gleams

To be what she was meant

A Place called home

That would make her whole

She found amidst flaring chrome

Within the depths of her own soul.

***

11.

All that of felt and All that of realised

All that of said and All that of never spoken

All that of observed and All that of known

All that of broken and All that of healing

All that of sadness and All that of happiness

All that of weakness and All that of strength

All that of darkness and All that of light

All that of ranting and All that of musings

All that of seasons and All that of reasons

All that of lies and All that of truth

From All the tunes of her soul

From All the strings of her heart

All that of thoughts She relates and

All that of words She writes

She's all of a Poet with her Poems

She's all of a Writer with her Proses.

***

12.

The most beautiful thing about her is not her looks,

 or her smile but, the confidence she wears even when she is broken inside!

***

13.

She re-incarnated

from her heart's explosion

In to that of a beautiful dark sky,

Illuminating brighter and shinier

For her heart is a Galaxy

Full of stars, dust and dark matter.

***

14.

Of the stars, the moon, the sun,

Of the sky, the oceans, the greens,

Of the blues and yellow, red hues,

She is a beautiful abstract,

Of what it is, the looks and the feels,

The burning fire within,

The depth, the coolness,

The shine, the warmth, and the mystery,

She is the metaphor of Nature,

Holds everything that a dreamer dreams of,

The thinker manifests in,

The magician entices,

Though one believes or not,

She's in You, and in all

That of power of love,

And of survivor of chaos!

***

Mixed Emotions:

One on all kinds!

1.

Feelings known with empathy

Love known only truly

Pain absorbed deeply

Joy conveyed genuinely

With pain so soul stirring

Still a profound kind being

Even when they are hurting

They are always caring

And Even though they are down

They still buckle down

To show great compassion

When needed without hesitation

Because that's how empaths are!

True, deep, kind, and giving with no bar!!

***

2.

Sometimes I wish

You were a lie too

Just like your love.

***

3.

Silence that haunts you

Sometimes becomes all the memory

You have and all the answers you need!

Silence… if you love it!

It will love you back!

Sometimes its all the aid you need and

All the peace you will find.

***

4.

When life's your teacher
Your hardships, your lessons
World, your pathway
Maturity, your experience
Then Young or Old
Your age doesn't matter
But the Wisdom, does.
Share. Spread. Connect. Inspire.
For that's what makes life worth living.

***

5.

When I listen to your

Favorite songs!

I can hear your voice,

I can feel your tone,

I can see your expressions,

All Playing in front of me,

The way you used to sing alone!

That makes me think,

You are always with me,

But its not the same,

I will always miss you,

I wish you never left,

I wish I told you every day,

How much I love you…

When I had a chance to!

But I know you always knew,

And kind of know even now,

That I did and I still do.

Always remember you!

***

6.

One last time, before I go!
One last time, in all, with all the time left!
One last time, before its all over!
One last time, one last try!
One last time, with all the temps!
One last time, one last chance!
One last time, to figure it all!
One last time, just one more time!
One last time, to be or May not be!
One last time, to have or May not have!
One last time, at all the odds!
One last time, to one time of new and old peeps!
One last time, maybe to lose!
One last time, maybe to see if it lasts!
One last time, for this time can never be back!
One last time, for this time might be the last time!

***

7.

Why do people set wrong expectations?

Why is the world so unreal and cruel?

There are stories being said of happily forever

Then there is the reality of just being forever

Despite of knowing the reality

Why do they create such surreal picture of life?

When they know there's gonna be hurt, pain and bad experiences

Why do they set up such illusional hopes?

Of what is gonna happen will not happen or

Just what happens the way it's bound to happen

Why is there such blind love shown?

When they are going to keep you in dark

Why do they make you believe?

When there is no base to keep hold of what is been said

Why the conditions are so made that?

When They know what they want but they don't act

Because of fear? because of unexpected expected failures?

Why are even people given hearts?

When they can't take control of their own feelings

Are people just destined to live in distress? living but suffocating?

Or all this complex tension being created by people for blocking happiness, love, and peace forever...!!!?

And yet they still show it off as Happily("Surviving") forever!

***

8.

There's an urge to smile

There's an urge to get lost

An urge to fall in love and

Float in the feeling of being lost

An urge to speak out infinite

Connecting the infinity

An urge to be silent and

Just stay lost in thoughts

Then there's an urge to travel

Travel to the places

That makes you smile

Makes you fall in love

Makes you connect to infinite

Makes you just stay silent and stay lost

Makes you float in the feeling of being lost

And makes you indefinitely speak about it

A feeling that's stronger than Wanderlust

A feeling of urge to never stop - ***"Fernweh"***

***

9.

Every day we wait for the Sun to rise, to set then the moon to rise along with the twinkling stars and every time we look at them we get lost in awe. We look upon the same sky that holds them all along with the clouds that sometimes disappears, sometimes pours rain, snows, or growls with thunders and storms, despite all those odds of its own the sky still holds them beautifully. Now the point is not whether there are 10 other Suns or Moons or even the Universe itself but of the one that we are in, living, looking at, experiencing and still waiting devotedly for that one Sun, to look at the same Moon and stars everyday but still never miss a chance to have a glimpse of them, the formation of clouds, the drizzling rains or even the clear sky, we simply fall in love with and wait for & never be bore of it, or that one place that our heart longs to even when we have travelled to lot many other places and visited more than once, that one special corner at a coffee place or a cosy space where we live, or like that one friend out of 100's of them, we have had or known, is there one such person in your life? No matter how many relationships you have had, that one human, you could live with and couldn't live without at the same time? Just like Sky, with whom you would wanna be despite Storms, like the place which is near to your heart that after you retire at whatever age, you will go there, stay and just be there! That one person with whom even not being at a place you call home you still feel home! If there is, all I say is to be loyal & honest, which I couldn't stop wondering why is it so hard to understand of old generations or new but are scattering away from that very idea and concept of authenticity despite vulnerabilities and hence slowly the bond, love, trust is slipping and vanishing away. You see even the Sky has a Land for it, that holds up too, with their nature of beautiful elements and destructive vulnerable side's, they both meet at a place, of which no one knows, they are just there, and nobody even has to ever know when they are clearly transparent to one another and are together HOME to each other.

***

10.

It's strange to feel so much on the inside and sometimes to Feel nothing on the outside! Maybe that's what being numb is and Maybe that's why few of us are tagged as weird because we feel too much but are afraid to be open about it! But maybe, if we lived exactly how we felt on inside and connected to the outer side at the same level! Maybe, just maybe we would have shown each other what we really are and when we don't feel anything anymore, we would know it too, that way even though there would have been pain but it would ache a little less, even though the hearts would have been broken but the brokenness, a little less, even though there would be dark times but the darkness, a little less, and of everything even though there wouldn't be love anymore but hopelessness, a little less. Maybe the whole point of being vulnerable and real is to feel the true state of being in love and get hurt a little less, even though it lasts a little less than ever, it would still feel like forever, just like the filaments inside a light bulb. Burning inside, incandescent on the outside, but feels the same cold when it's off, and same hot when it's on, inside-out!

***

11.

You laugh because

You made me fool

I laugh because

You let go

Something that's true.

***

12.

Perceptions! Misconceptions!
Rightish wrongs connections!
Sugar coated lies,
Defaming stories!
Of gossips and rumours,
That grows like Tumors!
Cannot shake the grounds,
Even if it creates wounds!
With infinite static power,
And a soulful conscious aura!
That creates and transforms,
Universe of the energies!
Pushes away the fake ness,
Embraces the raw ness!
Fearless and boldness,
Anti-Senseless prejudices!
Opinions of rightfulness,
Advocate of justices!
Values of truth and freedom
On the path taken seldom
If it has to, be alone,
I choose to stand alone!
Stand tall and strong, alone!
For sometimes to do great things,
You have to take a small step,
Even if it means to walk alone,
Passing energies to grow and clone!

***

13.

Superpower as a Writer...
I hold the power of words and
I can emphasize on the volume of my voice and
I can hear the echo from other side of the world and around in sync!
And we can together make it heard!
Make the truth roar!
My words can be the thunder and show light to wade away through the darkest clouds and
My voice like the rain, felt by those who don't mind getting drenched by it and
Keep on walking on the path of justice!
And we shall prevail over the darkest times and make our way until the sun rises and shines again!
For this is my way of fighting,
Driving through the path of Humanity asking justice for all!
Empowering and channeling through different mediums in small steps, one at a time!!
Until senses that "crime has no religion" is imbibed in each human!

***

14.

As I opened the eyes
So did the night with dawn
Just with the sunrise
My pain in the heart rose too
Like the rays shined out of the sky
The wounded scars inside etched too
As the day went by with sunny brightness
My head was filled with gloomy thoughts
As the clouds began to hover over the sky
The memories of our togetherness hovered over me
With the lightening thunders and the stormy weather
The pain came out as shouts and tears rolled down
It then rained, rained heavily and beautifully
But my eyes rained too uncontrollably vulnerably
As the sunset hid behind all the darkness
All my smiles did too with a dark dark shadow
As the night came by and as the moon rose
Somehow the demons came out and close
The night grew darker with darkest clouds
The demons grew stronger with longing growls
Just like the day ended and sun moon and stars drowned
My strength and conscious in my bones and blood drowned too...
Next day I opened my eyes...Again.
So did the night with dawn...Again.

***

15.

She always loved Life

But it betrayed her many a times

When she lost hopes on it

She crushed on to the Death

She madly longed for it

But it never wanted her,

Somehow Life turned up to her again

She fell in love with it again

Started believing In new dreams

With new hopes and high spirits

Ironically It was in that moment

When Death fell hard for her

And before she could kiss Life

Death passionately kissed her,

Taking her away from Life, Forever!

***

16.

Artist and Writer are two of a kind.

One paints colours on a blank canvas

One scribbles words on a blank paper.

Constantly in search, Of that holds

And of what frees their soul

Both, create art from their blank thoughts.

Deciphered by a few, sometimes,

But always misinterpreted by many.

***

17.

Regret feels like an injection

Painfully injected deep

But when the drug finally

Acts on Infection, it heals!

***

18.

When I go back to counting

the years that i have known you,

I somehow end up sensing

the feel of knowing you the longest,

and hence stirring all the rush of pain

again, for a little more longer!

***

19.

In a parallel universe, Somewhere above,

The worlds perceptions, theories and histories,

Between a girl and a boy, Depending on,

How they look

How they style

How they bleed

Hope there is no difference,

Of Their shape, structure or size

But are stated, treated and believed

As an equal being, In everything they do

With no question of Gender restrictions,

Of age, position and wage.

A free parallel universe

Where a girl isn't killed for a boy

Or tortured, damaged and killed by a boy

Where she isn't a sex object

Where she isn't just some flesh

Where she isn't more of a target

For abuse, assault and violence

Where she isn't a burden or shame

But pride and of equal stature

As that of a boy and every being,

Treated as equal as deserving

Like that as the "Adishakti" •

Hopefully someday maybe

Everything that is being

Fought, stood and lead for

Will soon be true in this universe.

***

20.

We are same, but not

We are different, but not

You are me and I am you, truly not

I am me and you are you, maybe not

There's everything related, also not

Everyone knows it, deeply not

Some understand this some may not... Just yet!

***

21.

Blank Page becomes

Broken soul's companion of...

Love, Pain, and,

Everything in between.

***

22.

Memories, either cheer you up or haunt you!

In the places you have created good times

In the places you have been let down

All those special moments and

All those not so special ones

Painful memories make you suffer like only you feel the pain

Cheerful ones makes you miss few

You try to sedate to forget the painful ones and

You try to get high on the cheerful ones

But sometimes the pain overtakes the good and all you can do is overwrite the good over pain!

Memories, strange to be true but are real!

***

23.

A lot more than half of her

She lost in him

And the rest

In the darkness

Being no more herself.

***

24.

The wrong ones are treated right! And,
The right ones are being hurt, by fools.
Emotionally traumatised, Mentally abused.,
Based on the shady toxicity overplayed as right
by the wrong one on to those fools who believe it! And,
When they have the right one they treat them as shit!!!
For the only fault of the right ones being that
They love in all the right ways and
give their all to such delusional fool
only to end up as a broken & damaged soul!

***

25.

Their Love never made its way
Because...
She got only pain, and,
He got her love but his ego won!

***

26.

You say you love her, but how have you shown her? For the words are fantasy and create a world that ain't there. She believed your words, but it was really just words and nothing else. Because you didn't act on your words. And after all, maybe you too know that words don't mean anything if they don't match with your actions.

Well, there comes the point for everyone and Where they are out of their illusions, which Your love was for her. She came closer to you believing your words but sadly your actions pushed her away from you.

***

27.

Coding and decoding

A new way to communicate to you

My feelings in a new language that you understand

But on process of transmitting the information

The decrypt was never encrypted by you

And it always remained as a code

That was never received, but bugged forever!

***

28.

You & I

Are just like

The Ocean & The Sky

Seem so near

Reflecting each other,

All the time,

Yet so very far

And Could never meet.

***

Last – I promise!:

One where it all's done!

(Inspirations and light

small poems)

1.

There can be a million side-stories!

But there will be only one-side

Of the story that will

Always remain so,

The true side!

***

2.

I make words. Words in relativity.

Where I frame my lies.

Of how I have forgotten you.

When the truth lies in its reflection.

***

3.

It's the simple little things that matter in life. Sometimes when you don't find joy anywhere, you create it in those simple little things. And The little things that give you joy aren't just a simple thing, anymore.

Like the smiling kids are a perfect example of how you can create joy with anything, at any time, at any place you want.

***

4.

When I go through

Heart breaking stuff

Stuff that gets me down

That literally sinks my heart

When all the gloomy clouds

Dance over my head

When the tears pours

From my eyes like rain

Also, when i wanna avoid

All the unwanted talks

You were always there for me

You make me smile

You make me giggle and

Even laugh like a loon!

Thank you for existing

In all your acts & toons.

~ *Dedications to comic world*~

***

5.

"Lost" in "Life in Technicolor"

With "A Rush of blood to the head"

When "Death and all his friends"

Stopped by, being "Politik"

In the "Clocks" of "Midnight"

"Hypnotised" me into "Ghost Stories"

You, like "The Scientist" swirl "Ink"

In "Yellow" singing to me

"I will try to fix you"

Playing "In my place" said

"Every teardrop is a waterfall"

It's okay that it "Hurts like Heaven"

When it's "True love"

Showed "Paradise" with

"A Sky full of stars"

Took me on "Adventure of a lifetime"

Lit "Sparks" "Always in my head"

With "Hymn for the weekend"

Lifting my spirits "Up&Up"

Yes, I will "Call it Magic"

Call you "Someone Special" A "Miracle"

And I needed "Something just like this"

~Dedication to Coldplay~

***

6.

Sometimes all you need is just a little push! What is the little push?

It is solely defined by you alone. Sometimes it can be words of someone you admire or of some stranger you haven't even met. Sometimes it's in those little comments on how much it inspired, how much it's appreciated, how much relatable it is or how beautifully it's been put, that can be that little push to keep one going and doing what they have been doing with a little more enthusiasm. Never doubt the power of your words of appreciation! It might mean just words to you but it would mean the world to a writer/an artist!

***

7.

Often, we get lost in search of peace! In search of what that brings in us the feeling of belonging, something that we can call our home. But only when you travel you realise home isn't a place but a feeling that breathes peace.

***

8.

To stay calm and maintain focus when you are lured by the darkness is the state of mind attained with a higher perspective. For when you perceive darkness otherwise, it's just the shadow of the light.

***

9.

"...Erase your identity and who are you?.,"

Take off the mask and what are you? What are you when you ain't the one you know, you are?

What are you when you have no courage?

Take out the fears and what are you?

Let go all the loved ones and who are you? Who are you when you don't know how things work? Who are you when you don't have things to work? Let go all the persons you met too and who are you?

Erase your memories and what makes you? What makes you, you, without your dreams? What makes you, without the hopes and goals? Erase your identity and what makes you, you?

Without a home and where are you? Where are you without your name? Where are you without any connection? Without any love and where are you?

So what defines you as you? What defines you, If you don't have any emotions? What defines you, If you don't have any conscious? So tell me, who are you and what really are you, or what makes you, and what defines you as "YOU" without "The You" - is it the truth or a lie?

***

10.

I am the painted colours,

The sketch of pastels & charcoal!

I am the expression;

The impression of thoughts!

Few get lost in me,

Few never get me!

I am what they fill in the

|B L A N K • C A N V A S|

I love the way I look,

I always wanna be such!

While I am in them & you,

They call me - The {A R T}

***

11.

And we are but just a particle of matter, space and galaxies of supremacy,

Around and everywhere,

Of all that we see and can't

Can sense and can't

Of which we are but

It's mosaic, just like the nature,

A beautiful Art! And our egos?

Well! A Tiny Spectacle of that particle,

Can't stand a chance anywhere.,

To exist! It only does to you, falsely,

Only until you choose,

The path of enlightenment!

***

12.

Sometimes nothing makes sense!!! Friendships, relationship, you, people, work, what you achieved, what you can achieve, happiness, food, old things, new things, wants, what's and why's, any damn thing, just nothing, nothing makes sense!!! But still, you just keep going on... Have to keep going!!!! Because you never know maybe, maybe someday, it will all make sense!!

***

13.

New day, new journey,

with the rays of sunrise

may there be new ways

for all to rise and shine!!!

***

14.

Sometimes

we try to find

Inspiration

in someone else's

Words.

And sometimes

Our words become

Someone else's

Inspiration.

***

15.

Writers and Poets, Live Forever.

They never die even after they are gone

Because they will always be remembered

In the imprints of every word of theirs

Written through the depth of their soul,

With every inch of their heart,

And every nerve of their brain,

They leave behind the legacy of letters

To relate, feel, inspire and to fascinate

Hence becoming Immortal and Eternal!

~Dedication for the Writers~

***

16.

"I am love!
I am the reason for life!
For I am a feeling!
A connection!
I don't want to be the reason for
war, deaths and hatred!
I don't want to be differentiated
with any factors!
And what is a human without a feeling!
Feel is what derives living,
Like the breath that you take,
I am in you and you are because of me!
For I am love, so are you!
Love is simply love!
Same gender or not!
Same race or not!
Same age or not!
With no discriminations
No definitions
Sometimes with no reasons at all!!
Love is for all!!
Let's not divide,
but be a pride tribe!"

…Every other day we come across the news that people are being treated with injustice, abused, mocked, killed, or are killing themselves because their love is not being accepted, or their love doesn't fit in someone else's box of rules, due to differences in their race, caste, religion, status, age, and/or of loving someone of the same gender!!
Who gave anyone the right to dictate how and whom one should love and not! You can control how much you feel love but you can't control the feeling itself!
When you can't stop doing something that you love, don't try to dictate someone to stop loving someone! Especially when they are choosing someone out of love in their full senses and awareness! No one has control over what they feel for, for sure they can

control their actions on it but shouldn't we all just have the freedom to choose with whom we feel connected, and want to be with, despite all the said factors, why should there even be a factor! TBH It's between the two of them to define their own factors of love and none of any damn person's business at the first place!!

"Love is a feeling & Without any emotion there won't be any purpose for life!
When living beings can be of all kinds, why can't love be of all kinds?

Love is universal and for the matter of fact love is the only reason we are all here!!!

You can try to oppose all you want but, in the end, Love wins!"

***

17.

Maybe we are supposed to be broken

So the light entrapped in the esoteric soul

Escapes out of those fissures

Shining bright like sunshine

Over the seeds of pain effectuated

Deep inside that dreamy heart

Sprouting them into beautiful flowers

Reminding the essence of love

And sign of strength in growing wise.

***

18.

Change happens when you first accept your mistakes/faults.

That's is how you learn and

try to correct it or avoid doing it again.

That's is how you grow and be a better person.

***

19.

When you think

You can't do it

Do it then!!! Especially then!!!

Just one last try!

With everything that you have!

Because... sometimes...

that one try is all that matters!!!

***

20.

Infinity! What is infinity? Why does it resemble butterfly theory? Or Earth's Magnetic field? Or Magic no. 8? Or conjoined zeroes? The mirror effects? The concentric flow of circles merged!! What was infinity? How did we come to that term? And how did we reach so far? Starting from Alphabets to learning the words, creating terms how it is and look at where we stand now! How did it all begin? Where did life start from? Who are we? Are we, as based on one of many scientific theories, outgrown microorganisms of a water body? Or are we byproducts of the evolution of the Ape Family? Or going by mythological theories are we some beings just appeared as a result of some mantras? Or are we all connected to Adam and Eve? Or actually an Alien generation that invaded on a planet and called it Earth! Or maybe we are all robots functioning in a stimulating environment controlled by someone with superior powers, some person or Alien or God? Who knows! TBH we don't know where we exactly originated from! How life began! How it all started!! It's all just wonderful idea of possibilities of what we are! And let's suppose and believe we were to be a speck of particle from universe resulting out of a collision and due to some element, it all began - the life! Then what is death? And if we are tiny specks of particles of a very minute part in the vast vast universe(s) then why all the EGO? Why all the hatred? Differences! Discriminations! Inferior and superior and unnecessary competitions? Why such stark opposites? Like good and bad? Why all the nuisances and evil spread? Maybe it is truly something related to the magnetic study that we know of, opposites exist and opposites attract "vibes"., While the same ones repel they do come together for a moment at a midpoint. And what is our purpose? Going by spirituality, we are spirits wandering of purpose to know ourselves and reach highest consciousness levels, and we attain infinity within each of us, then why do we need to prove something and have all the comparisons among us instead of compassion and Love? They say Love is also Infinity! So, are we also love? Maybe we are all just Magic!

***

Surprise:

cuz you are special

(Quotes)

She was one of those

Rare wild wild souls

She either wanted the whole damn Universe

or just nothing at all

***

Sure, it looks beautiful! But if u keep looking what's behind, you will miss the beauty of what's now and ahead!! And Maybe it is and it's gonna be even more beautiful than what it was because YOU know and CAN make it always BETTER than what it WAS!!

Of past and reflections.

***

There's something about the Window seats.

A place where you get lost

In the realms of thoughts.

***

The tiny spark of light in darkness

Lead all the way to the soul!

***

Some conversations take you on time travel from just nowhere to alternate dimensions when it's done about things that matter with the one that matter.

***

Time is the creator of the endless stories of this life! And we are all mere travellers on a voyage to discover our purpose and ultimately learn what Time had to teach.

***

Some words are like

The King of the jungle

They Roar Wild thoughts!

***

Hoping for a New day, Sailing through the turbulent winds, smiling through the waves of troubles at the end of the day in a beautiful way. Flight of Hope it is

***

Bloom Beautifully like a Flower in this beautiful world! Also, grow some thorns and be fucking Wild in this beautiful fucking world!

***

Writing is what relates, not just fancy words!

So is love!!

***

We create our own living hells

By feeling guilty for madly loving

someone who never loved us the same!

***

Equality feels like the first ray of Sun

Touching the horizon after the darkest night!

***

Maybe the whole purpose of life is to attain supremacy of oneself to unlock the next journey called death, which maybe is just another new level of life!

***

I think we are not put on earth

To find the perfect match for ourselves, but,

To find someone who makes perfect sense

To be together even with the Imperfections!

***

What are we after all? Different ships sailing in the large ocean to the unknown destinations trying to find that one perfect place, to harbour and if it gives solace., to live there till the end in peace..!!

***

Love is "Sunset" for it beautifies everything with its orange & red hues.

***

Self-Love should be a daily reminder!

Your daily dose of magic to yourself!

***

Follow the light within, it enlightens the soul!

***

When u don't know what to do anymore and can't fix anything!! You just calm yourself by reading such fictional stories!!!

***

The Dark side of Love!!!

The more it hurts the more darker it grows...

nothing can fade the darkness,

but Only Love!

***

The beauty of life is creating a galaxy of happiness in little things!

***

Distance between hearts is the farthest of all the longest miles!

And one who understands this will go miles crossing the farthest distance for the longest time!

***

Sometimes among everything bright & shiny around... You end up being alone!

***

Life is like going on a long drive to some unknown destination,

where you have many diversions which will confuse you,

but if you notice carefully you also have

Signs to take you on the right path!

***

The best thing about photograph is you create a time stamp of the moment which you lived and could live again wherever you want to.

***

Windows everywhere is a magical place for thoughts to evoke.

***

If you can't find a window of opportunity, create one!

***

"Let's be fireflies and let our inner light be the language of our love."

***

"Let's get high on spirits among the lights, and get lost swinging to the tunes to eternal world."

***

Anyone can shine when the sun shines!

But only the one with inner light, can shine in the darkest nights even without the moonlight!

***

We are all a little broken in the inside! But how we perceive life, defines our brokenness! We all fight a battle to get through it, while some hide themselves behind it, and others hide it gently with their smiles!

***

Moon shines from within

For itself, but that shine

Guides everyone through the darkness,

Brightens the whole damn sky!

While letting the stars to twinkle too.

***

Pixie dust

You are awesome!

1.

I rise above destruction!

I fly, I grow, I balance

I hold on to my roots.

I see things, I find peace,

I go beyond of what it is.

I pause, I live, I relive

The moments, The rain

The shine of day and night.

I hold the light, the darkness,

All the colours in between.

I am time, I am space,

I am blank, I am whole,

I have nothing that I own,

I am creator of my own!

***

2.

In the darkest hour

Even when you constantly fight

There will be a weakest moment

Do not let it overpower you

Do not let it make you vulnerable

Even if it did, do not feel lonely

Reach out your hand

And allow yourself to be hold

Do not let it make you believe

Nobody cares, cuz they do.

You are not alone!

Fight! Talk! And It shall pass...

For only after the darkest hour,

The blue skies are visible clearer.

You are the Goddamn Sky!

That holds Sun, Moon, & Stars,

Dark and Silver lined Clouds,

Thunders, Rains and Storms!

Holds Everything in between,

Evolves in Beautiful Hues.

And Darling, you are all that!

You are not just enough,

You are Everything! Believe it!

***

3.

Through every Stoke of thunder,

Every drop of rain,

Through every rays of sunlight

And warmth of moonlight,

You grow,

If you allow yourself to get through...

If you let yourself face with all the adversities and goodness,

You transform just like seed to flower and

Finally to what it's ought to be...

Itself!

Unique and Complete!

***

4.

Hey you! Pretty girl! Its ok be mad! Be sad! Cry out your heart if that makes you feel light. Have a tub of ice cream, eat tons of chocolates, don't sleep, maybe don't eat, or overeat, don't go anywhere, if you don't feel like. Stay in, stay lazy in your bed, its fine, maybe don't talk to anyone about how you feel! Just be, just stay, just forget the world, overthink about stuff that you think shouldn't have gone wrong which should have gone right if done in right way. Connecting this to that. But when you are finally done. Get over it. Like in all the bloody ways. Flush it all out of your system. Till then take your own sweet time, To get back to all your normal ways or maybe new ways. But do me a favour will you? And never ever forget that "You are beautiful And You deserve so much more and better than you even know." Say this to yourself every day, maybe?

And the rest.. Well it shall pass and you shall shine brighter than ever. Just never stop believing yourself!

And So do you pretty boy!

***

5.

They call you Mad! Because you follow your passion. Because you go after what your heart wants. Because you get going at it, crazy, with no difference of night or day, like you have no idea of what the clock says or the calendar, just at it on a spree to give a shape to your ideas, to your thoughts! You become unstoppable and what it is to normal, "Insane"! Because they see the spark in your eyes for what you love and most of the times you are zoned out into your own galaxy of cerebration, which streams like a series of different perspectives you hold or new, what it is to normal, "Delusional"! So you don't make sense to anyone but someday your work will and what's the fun in being normal anyway? Embrace your madness! Keep it alive!

Because beautiful, that's what your real beauty is!

***

6.

I Am!

But everything

that you know of!

And that you don't know!

In your heart

In your mind

In everything you see

In everyplace you go

Connected to your soul

Always!

Even when you drift apart

Or when you get closer

Even if you love or hate

In all your words and thoughts

I Am!

***

7.

You know what? I get you! No, Really! I do!

You think about the people and the people who were dear to you once, The ones you trusted, You think you got ditched, but you didn't! You got saved!

You think your light is being dimmed, but no one can! Because it's within you! Always!

You think you can't fight them, but you need not! Because you already won, whilst they were trying to pull you down!

You think you have been played, you didn't! You were too nice, that you didn't doubt their intentions!

You think all your Hard work has gotten in vain, it didn't! Because everything has its own time!

You think you have been hated, but you are not! You are being secretly admired for they can't be You or can't have what you do!

You feel sad, you feel the pain and you protect yourself with a higher ego, so that, no one can touch your sensitivity, no one can reach your vulnerability, and, No one can hurt you ever or make you feel any less...

But dear, how will you be YOU? and how will you make your dreams come true without being your own self!?

So, disengage yourself from what they did, what you did, forgive them, forgive yourself but don't forget what you went thru, don't fill yourself with overprotective ego, be kind to others but first to yourself.

Because Maybe you might lose on the right one, by not allowing them to have the privilege of being with the real you! The good side of you, the nicer you!

Give them a chance! Give yourself a chance!

Change to change yourself from the change that changed you to real and better you!

And don't you worry of your dreams, your time will come and time shall follow you, when you have the right attitude and Consistent focus on right things and with the right one beside you, right things will happen!!! Definitely!

You are a Work-In-Process and I am with you in it! Because I believe you.

***

THANK YOU VERY MUCH FOR READING MY WRITINGS!!

Hope the "BIT OF SOUL" got connected from mine to yours!

PLEASE feel free to share your most liked writing of mine and spread the word about it!

www.ingramcontent.com/pod-product-compliance
Lightning Source LLC
Chambersburg PA
CBHW031316160426
43196CB00007B/552